Understanding Globalization, Global Gaps, and Power Shifts in the 21st Century

Huiyao Wang · Lu Miao
Editors

Understanding Globalization, Global Gaps, and Power Shifts in the 21st Century

CCG Global Dialogues

palgrave
macmillan

Editors
Huiyao Wang
Center for China and Globalization
(CCG)
Beijing, China

Lu Miao
Center for China and Globalization
(CCG)
Beijing, China

ISBN 978-981-19-3848-1   ISBN 978-981-19-3846-7   (eBook)
https://doi.org/10.1007/978-981-19-3846-7

This Palgrave Macmillan imprint is published by the registered company Springer Nature Singapore Pte Ltd.
The registered company address is: 152 Beach Road, #21-01/04 Gateway East, Singapore 189721, Singapore

PREFACE

As part of our mission to serve as a bridge between China and the rest of the world, each year the Center for China and Globalization (CCG) hosts a range of speakers from around the world at its headquarters in Beijing. We have also worked to build various bespoke channels and platforms to enhance dialogue between scholars, business leaders, policymakers, and young people from China and abroad. This includes an annual program of seminars, workshops, and flagship events such as the China and Globalization Forum and the Inbound-Outbound Forum. Representatives of CCG also participate in international events to exchange views with people around the world.

As part of these efforts, at the Munich Security Conference in February 2020, CCG held a discussion on China–US relations and co-hosted a roundtable on maritime security to consult with counterparts from the US and elsewhere on these key issues. As it turned out, this conference was to prove one of the last major in-person international events before the world was turned upside down by COVID-19. Subsequently, international meetings and diplomatic summits were canceled in quick succession as borders closed and cross-border travel ground to a halt.

Right when the world was facing a global health and economic crisis that called for dialogue and cooperation, many of the usual channels of interaction between people from different countries closed down. As the pandemic spread and geopolitical tensions rose, there was a greater need than ever for calm, rational discussion to share views, make sense of the momentous changes that were occurring, and find ways to work together.

As life was interrupted for everyone around the world and many countries endured rolling lockdowns, like everyone else, CCG worked to adapt to these new circumstances. We reached out to old friends and new to set up dialogues in a virtual format which allowed us to speak with leading experts around the world from CCG's new multimedia center in Beijing via video link. Although we were often separated by thousands of miles, twenty-first-century technology allowed us to converse in real-time and even lent a certain "fireside chat" intimacy to our virtual dialogues as participants spoke unscripted and candidly from their own homes and offices in various continents.

When we started the CCG Dialogue Series, we had no idea what course the pandemic would take and when in-person meetings would resume. We were eager to converse with experts from different countries and disciplines that could help us put current events in context and explore solutions to our shared challenges. The series continued to develop, attracting audiences of hundreds of thousands of viewers in China and abroad. The list of participants grew to include prominent journalists and authors, Nobel laureates, former officials with extensive experience at the highest levels of government and multilateral institutions, and world-renowned scholars in fields such as international relations, economics, and trade.

Since launching the CCG Global Dialogue Series in 2021, we have found the perspectives that participants have shared with us to be invaluable in helping to understand the trends reshaping our world. The discussions have also generated many ideas as to how we might work together to forge a post-pandemic world that is peaceful, prosperous, and more inclusive. After these conversations took place, these ideas have only come to seem more timely and important as the war in Ukraine brings a tragic reminder of what can happen when we fail to work together. Therefore, we were eager to share these talks in the form of a book so that readers could absorb the insights shared by our speakers, compare and contrast their perspectives, and enhance their understanding of important issues such as globalization, global governance and multilateralism, the global economy, our shared transnational threats, and China–US relations.

It is in this spirit that CCG has compiled this collection of discussions from the CCG Dialogue Series that took place between March and

October 2021. At a time when international politics has become more contentious and polarized than ever, we hope this collection will help readers develop a nuanced and balanced understanding of some of these crucial themes of our times.

We are exceptionally grateful to all of the discussants that participated in the CCG Dialogue Series and allowed for their comments to be republished in this collection. Without their inspiration, insights, and generosity, this publication would have never been possible. In particular, we would like to extend our warmest thanks to the following speakers in chronological order of their participation in this dialogue series: Kerry Brown, Director of the Lau Institute, King's College London (March 2, 2021); Thomas L. Friedman, author and New York Times Op-Ed columnist (March 29, 2021); Graham Allison, Douglas Dillon Professor of Government at Harvard University and Chen Li, Director of the Center for International Security and Strategy at the School of International Studies, Renmin University of China (April 6, 2021); Joseph S. Nye Jr., Harvard University Distinguished Service Professor, Emeritus (April 28, 2021); Martin Wolf, Chief Economics Commentator at the Financial Times (May 12, 2021); Anne Case, Alexander Stewart 1886 Professor of Economics and Public Affairs, Emeritus at Princeton University and Angus Deaton, Senior Scholar, Princeton School of Public and International Affairs (May 13, 2021); Valerie Hansen, Stanley Woodward Professor of History at Yale University (May 17, 2021); Adam S. Posen, President of the Peterson Institute for International Economics, J. Stapleton Roy, Founding Director Emeritus, Kissinger Institute on China and the United States, former United States Ambassador to China, John L. Thornton, Chair Emeritus at the Brookings Institution and Co-Chair of the Asia Society, and Zhu Guangyao, CCG Advisor and former Vice Minister of Finance of China (July 30, 2021); Wendy Cutler, Vice President at the Asia Society Policy Institute and former Acting Deputy US Trade Representative and Pascal Lamy, President of the Paris Peace Forum and former Director-General of the World Trade Organization (August 2, 2021); and Kishore Mahbubani, Distinguished Fellow at the Asia Research Institute, National University of Singapore and former Singaporean Ambassador to the UN (October 19, 2021). I would also like to express my deepest appreciation to audiences in China and abroad that have helped to make this CCG Dialogue series a success and to the staff at CCG for their hard work that made these events possible.

We hope the conversations in this volume will offer readers a rich spectrum of perspectives and provoke further thought and conversation on these important topics. A common thread in the discussions that follow is that while the post-pandemic era is full of tough challenges and uncertainties, there is also much scope for cooperation to overcome these challenges and many opportunities for mutual gain if the global community can work together. We firmly believe that candid, open discussion is the key to building mutual trust and facilitating deeper cooperation. We look forward to continuing our work through initiatives like the CCG Dialogue series, hoping that we can make some small contribution to building bridges and raising mutual understanding, so that we may be better able to look beyond our differences, better understand each other, and find ways to coexist peacefully and work together to overcome our most serious shared challenges.

Beijing, China   Dr. Henry Huiyao Wang
August 2022   Dr. Mabel Lu Miao

CONTENTS

EDITORS

Dr. Henry Huiyao Wang is the Founder and President of Center for China and Globalization (CCG), a think tank ranked among top 100 think tanks in the world. He is also Dean of the Institute of Development Studies of Southwestern University of Finance and Economics of China, Vice Chairman of China Association for International Economic Cooperation and a Director of Chinese People's Institute of Foreign Affairs. He is currently a steering committee member of Paris Peace Forum and an advisory board member of Duke Kunshan University. He has served as an expert for the World Bank, IOM, and ILO. He pursued his Ph.D. studies at the University of Western Ontario and the University of Manchester. He was Senior Fellow at Harvard Kennedy School and Visiting Fellow at Brookings Institute. His books in English include *Globalizing China* (2012); *China Goes Global* (2016); the *Handbook on China and*

Globalization (2019); the *Globalization of Chinese Enterprises* (2020); and *Consensus or Conflict?: China and Globalization in the 21st Century* (2021); *China and the World in a Changing Context: Perspectives from Ambassadors to China* (2022); and *The Ebb and Flow of Globalization* (2022).

Dr. Mabel Lu Miao is the Co-Founder and Secretary-General of CCG, a Munich Security Conference (MSC) Young Leader and the Founder of Global Young Leaders Dialogue (GYLD). She is also the Deputy Director-General of the International Writing Center at Beijing Normal University. She received her Ph.D. in contemporary Chinese studies from Beijing Normal University and has been a visiting scholar at New York University's China House and the Fairbank Center at Harvard University. She is a co-author of many Chinese Social Science Academy blue books and Chinese Social Science Foundation's research project reports. She has published a number of books in Chinese, which detail China's outbound business and global talent. Her latest publications in English are: *International Migration of China: Status, Policy and Social Responses to the Globalization of Migration* (2017); Blue Book of Global Talent; Annual Report on the Development of Chinese Students Studying Abroad; *China's Domestic and International Migration Development* (2019); and *Transition and Opportunity: Strategies from Business Leaders on Making the Most of China's Future* (2022).

Contributors

Graham Allison Harvard Kennedy School, Cambridge, MA, USA

David Blair Center for China and Globalization (CCG), Beijing, China

Kerry Brown Lau China Institute, King's College London, London, UK

Anne Case Princeton University, Princeton, NJ, USA

Wendy Cutler Asia Society Policy Institute (ASPI), Washington, DC, USA

Angus Deaton Princeton University, Princeton, NJ, USA

Thomas L. Friedman The New York Times, New York, NY, USA

Valerie Hansen Department of History, Yale University, New Haven, CT, USA

Pascal Lamy Paris Peace Forum, Paris, France

Chen Li Renmin University of China, Beijing, China

Kishore Mahbubani Asia Research Institute of National University of Singapore (NUS), Singapore, Singapore

Joseph S. Nye Jr. Harvard Kennedy School, Cambridge, MA, USA

Adam S. Posen Peterson Institute for International Economics (PIIE), Washington, DC, USA

J. Stapleton Roy Wilson Center, Washington, DC, USA

John L. Thornton Barrick Gold Corporation, Toronto, ON, Canada

Huiyao Wang Center for China and Globalization (CCG), Beijing, China

Martin Wolf Financial Times, London, UK

Zhu Guangyao Counsellor's Office of the State Council, Beijing, China

Introduction

Huiyao Wang and Lu Miao

A "Pale Blue Dot" Moment?

Two of the most iconic photographs ever taken show the Planet Earth from space. *The Blue Marble* was taken 29,000 kilometers from the Earth's surface on December 7, 1972. It was the first-ever photograph of the whole round Earth, introducing us to the astonishing beauty of our blue-green island in the vast black ocean of space. In the image, we can clearly see the continental landforms and oceans of the Earth, ranging from the Mediterranean, down through the green and brown swathes of the entire African continent, to the vast ice lands of the Antarctic shrouded in swirling white clouds.

Today, we are so used to images of Earth from space that it is perhaps difficult to recall the impact that the photo had at the time. For the first time, this planetary perspective allowed us to see the precious Earth that is the shared home of all of humanity. It was hoped the image might change how we related to the Earth and each other, reminding us of our shared

H. Wang (✉)
Center for China and Globalization (CCG), Beijing, China

L. Miao
Center for China and Globalization (CCG), Beijing, China

© The Author(s) 2022
H. Wang and L. Miao (eds.), *Understanding Globalization, Global Gaps, and Power Shifts in the 21st Century*, https://doi.org/10.1007/978-981-19-3846-7_1

1

destiny and how what we share in common far outweighs any differences that might exist between groups differentiated by nationality, language, religion, or ideology.

The second iconic image of Earth, *Pale Blue Dot*, was taken about 18 years later and leaves quite a different impression. While *The Blue Marble* shows the Earth in vivid color with its familiar coastlines and continents, in the *Pale Blue Dot*, taken around 6 billion kilometers away from Earth, our planet is a barely visible blue speck against the dark background of vast space. Of the 640,000 pixels that make up each frame of the *Pale Blue Dot*, Earth takes up less than one pixel. To paraphrase the astronomer Carl Sagan, it is humbling and sobering to look at this "mote of dust suspended in a sunbeam" and think of the wars that generals and emperors have waged through history, all for momentary control of a fraction of that pale blue dot. The vastness of the cosmic dark that surrounds Earth is also a reminder that our planet is the only viable home for our species, at least in the near future.

Images like *The Blue Marble* and the *Pale Blue Dot* force us to take a step back and adopt a more planetary perspective on the world we live in. As John L. Thornton reminded us in this dialogue series, when we see the Earth from space, there are no real differences between people living in China, the US, Africa, Europe, or elsewhere. Any boundaries between us are completely invisible.

The need to set aside our differences and adopt a more global perspective to overcome our shared challenges proved to be a recurring theme in this dialogue series, one that has only become more salient since this dialogue series began, given the continuing challenges of the pandemic, the tragic war in Ukraine, and the gradually unfolding climate crisis. Participants in this series used many vivid metaphors to emphasize the fundamental interdependence of humanity, such as the "global village" or how China and the US are "conjoined twins" destined to live or die together.

In the final dialogue in this book, Kishore Mahbubani uses the analogy of a boat. As Kishore said, in the past, when we thought of the global population living in 193 separate countries, it was as though they lived on 193 separate boats; each boat had a captain and crew to take care of it, and each boat was more or less independent. However, now that the world has shrunk due to globalization and our shared global challenges, while the global population of almost 8 billion people may live in 193 separate countries, we now see that they are no longer on 193 separate boats. Rather, we all live in 193 separate cabins on the same boat, and we must therefore take care of this shared boat together.

In many ways, the global outbreak of COVID-19 we experienced in early 2020 could have sparked a "pale blue dot moment"—a rare point in history when humanity had the chance to adopt a truly planetary perspective, recognize our shared interests and how we are truly all in the same boat, and put aside our quarrels to work together for the greater good. Like climate change, the pandemic is a prime example of a shared threat that pays no heed to national borders.

Unfortunately, that is not quite how things played out. Rather than spur global cooperation and show the enduring relevance of multilateralism, the pandemic did more to expose the fractures and fragilities of the current international system. In 2022, the international system was again found wanting as it proved unable to prevent war in Ukraine and the great human suffering and economic disruption that followed. A major theme and motivation of this dialogue series was to understand these global gaps and fragilities, the structural trends that have caused them, and to explore ways of rebuilding our societies and systems of global governance so we can emerge from this global crisis to build a world that is more cohesive, inclusive, and sustainable.

PART I: THE EVOLUTION OF GLOBALIZATION

In the early stages of the pandemic, some speculated that COVID-19 might be a death knell for globalization. Recent years had seen an uptick in anti-globalization sentiment and push back against the cross-border flow of goods, capital, and people, primarily in industrialized countries. As borders closed and trade flows contracted in the first half of 2020, there was a deluge of commentary announcing that we had passed "peak globalization." However, it soon became clear that, far from the end of globalization, the pandemic merely marked a new phase of this multi-dimensional process. In 2022, the war in Ukraine and unprecedented economic sanctions enforced against Russia again prompted some commentators to pronounce the "end of globalization." But this event too surely marks the beginning of a new chapter in which globalization will continue to adapt and evolve, rather than a fundamental halting of the process of global integration. The three dialogues in Part I of this book take a big picture view to trace the evolution of globalization from ancient history to its myriad forms today.

BACK TO THE YEAR 1000

When times are fraught and change occurs at a dizzying pace, the perspective of a historian is invaluable. Perhaps no one is better placed to give a long-term view of globalization than Valerie Hansen, Stanley Woodward Professor of History at Yale and renowned historian of China, the Silk Road, and early globalization.

The start of globalization is often dated to the first voyages of Christopher Columbus, who first made landfall in the Caribbean in 1492. In the first dialogue in this book, Hansen shares the main findings from her most recent book, *The Year 1000*, which builds a compelling case to date the start of globalization almost five centuries earlier, based on the explosion of trade, exploration, and cultural exchange that connected the world's great societies at the end of the first millennium. Her research shows how, since its earliest beginnings, the process of globalization has been driven by the universal human impulse to learn and acquire new things from around the world, an impulse that continues to drive globalization in its various forms today. In our discussion, Hansen paints a vivid picture of Song Dynasty China as being one of the most globalized places on earth in the year 1000, notable as a manufacturing center for exports, a major market for products imported from across the world, and a relatively open society that absorbed influences from many different cultures, religions, and schools of thought.

Lest we think that the current pushback against globalization is something new to our current era, Hansen recounts stories of riots against foreign merchants in Cairo in 996 and in Constantinople in the early 1180s, showing that while people have long benefitted from globalization, there have also always been groups that were harmed by it and wanted to restrain it. She points out that while early forms of globalization such as overland trade via the Silk Road or perilous maritime routes were always constrained by the forces of nature, these limitations have diminished with the advent of new technologies such as container ships and cargo planes. Hence, Hansen says it is important not to overlook the losers of globalization and that we must find ways to manage and lessen its negative impacts.

Multispeed Globalization

Bringing us forward to the present day, the second discussion in Part I features Martin Wolf, Chief Economic Commentator of the *Financial Times* and author of the acclaimed book *Why Globalization Works*. As Wolf points out, to understand how globalization is changing, rather than simply view it as a singular process, it is important to disaggregate its different components and look at the diverging trajectories they are taking.

For example, Wolf observes that one aspect of globalization, the unbundling of supply chains and cross-border movement of goods, may have reached a natural plateau. This is because, under current technological conditions, the opportunities to dice up and redistribute segments of supply chains have largely been exploited already. Key technologies that drive globalization have matured and changed little in recent decades; airplanes move basically as fast as they did 40 years ago, and the innovation of standard containerization is now almost 70 years old.

At the same time, Wolf notes that "virtual globalization" or the globalization of ideas still has vast potential to deepen interaction among human beings, powered by technologies such as 5G, the Metaverse, and Artificial Intelligence. This phenomenon of "multispeed globalization" has certainly been evident during the pandemic. While certain flows such as the movement of goods and people have been temporarily slowed, others have been turbocharged, such as cross-border data flows.

The World Is Fast, Fused, Deep, and Open

Thomas Friedman has become something of a poster child for globalization since the publication of *The World Is Flat* in 2005. The book argued that by the early twenty-first century, the world had become "flattened" by various economic, technological, and cultural forces.

At the start of my dialogue with Friedman, the third in Part I, he notes how people had asked him during webinars amidst the pandemic, "Is the world still flat?" To which his answer was, "Are you kidding? It's flatter than ever!" As evidence, he cites the very conversation we were having at the time, between himself in Bethesda, Maryland, and me in Beijing, talking in real-time via Zoom.

Updating his "world is flat" thesis for the 2020s, Friedman pithily sums up how globalization has now made our world "fast, fused, deep, and open." The world is "fast" because there has been a dramatic change in the pace of change. It is "fused" because the world is more interdependent than ever, fused by technology and the climate, in particular. The world is now "deep" because sensors and various forms of technology now permeate our world, equipping us with "deep" knowledge and allowing us to peer into other things and places using tools like Google Earth. Finally, Friedman says that the world has become radically "open" because devices like smartphones mean that any citizen is now a filmmaker, journalist, and a publisher, and can capture and transmit images across the world with no filter, as seen when the video of George Floyd went viral worldwide in May 2020.

Part II: Bridging Gaps and Deficits

The dialogues in Part I of this book map out some of the long-term structural trends and complex changes that have reshaped our world in recent decades. But while changes in technology, the global economy, and ecological processes have occurred rapidly, our policies, institutions, and mindsets have typically been slower to adapt. This mismatch between practice and reality has led to gaps opening up in several key areas. These gaps and deficits are the shared theme of discussions featured in Part II.

The current gaps in equality, institutions, and understanding are especially significant because they are interlinked and feed into each other. For example, domestic inequality can fuel populism and anti-globalization sentiment, hindering the reform of global institutions. North–south global inequality can impact cooperation on shared challenges like climate change. Gaps in understanding can cause citizens and policymakers to place too much emphasis on rivalry and certain perceived security risks when more attention should be paid to cooperating on larger transnational challenges.

The Equality Deficit

One of the many existing problems that the pandemic has exposed is the yawning inequality gap between countries. As Pascal Lamy points out in this dialogue series, nowhere is this more striking than in the uneven distribution of vaccines across the world, something he refers to as "vaccine apartheid." As Lamy says, this vaccine divide will significantly slow our exit from the pandemic and its associated economic crisis. It will also exacerbate the north–south divide, with consequences for our joint efforts to tackle other global problems, such as climate change negotiations.

Inequality is also serious and widening within many countries. A particular case of this divide in the US is highlighted in *Deaths of Despair and the Future of Capitalism*, a groundbreaking book authored by the speakers in the first dialogue of Part II, the economists Anne Case and Angus Deaton. In their conversation with me and CCG Vice President and Senior Economist David Blair, Case and Deaton describe how the US is unusual in having witnessed a reversal in the long-term trend of increasing life expectancy, with life expectancy actually falling from 2015 to 2017, a trend not seen elsewhere. During this period, the fastest rising death rates among Americans were from drug overdoses, suicide, and alcoholic liver disease. Research by Case and Deaton has shed light on the social and economic forces that have made life harder for less privileged groups in America and so contributed to these "deaths of despair." However, they point out that conventional stories about globalization and technological change cannot fully explain this phenomenon, as other industrialized countries have not experienced the same public health crisis. Instead, Case and Deaton highlight the significance of policy decisions related to income redistribution, worker retraining, and America's dysfunctional healthcare system that have made blue-collar workers more vulnerable to rapid changes in the economy and society.

The Institutional Deficit

Over the course of this dialogue series, a general consensus emerged that many of the most pressing problems we currently face, from the pandemic and climate change to trade frictions and the impact of the digital economy, can be linked to deficits in our global governance and institutions.

The system of global governance formed after the Second World War, largely the one that still exists today, was designed for a world in which a few powerful countries called the shots; a world in which national boundaries were all important and the most pressing problems arose within or between states. We now live in an increasingly digital and multipolar world linked by cross-border flows and global challenges, but our system of global governance has failed to keep up and adapt, in part because of a lack of leadership and consensus at the global level. This gulf between global governance and the realities of the twenty-first century has led to severe gaps in global institutions when it comes to areas like climate, the ability to undertake a coordinated international response to global health crises, and norms and rules to manage the digital economy.

In Part I, Martin Wolf links this global institutional gap to a fundamental tension between the logic of the economy, which is global and not deeply anchored nationally, and the logic of politics, which remains national. International government, such as it exists, essentially rests on the voluntary cooperation of national governments that rely on domestic legitimacy and accountability. As Wolf describes, this makes it difficult to maintain international cooperation among governments to create global order and update global institutions for things like trade, finance, or climate, because all the political forces acting on these institutions are national and so prioritize the narrower concerns of national citizens.

The gap in global institutions that has opened up in the twenty-first century is particularly evident when we look at the World Trade Organization (WTO). This topic is explored in-depth in the second dialogue in Part II with Wendy Cutler, Vice President of Asian Society Policy Institute and former Acting Deputy USTR, and Pascal Lamy, former WTO Director-General and President of the Paris Peace Forum.

As Lamy notes, while the global economy has changed dramatically since the 1990s, WTO rules have remained largely unchanged since then. This gap has resulted in frictions over new issues and an uptick in judicial activism in the dispute settlement mechanism as judges try to reinterpret old rules to match new realities. Both Lamy and Cutler link this failure of the WTO to reform itself to the machinery and processes by which the organization operates and makes decisions. In particular, the WTO remains a strongly member-driven organization compared to other international institutions, which has made it difficult to forge consensus and move forward. To overcome this, Lamy suggests that authority in the WTO should be rebalanced such that the director-general and secretariat can play a larger role in "co-driving" the organization along with the membership. Cutler recommends that more use be made of plurilateral agreements under which subsets of WTO members negotiate and reach agreements, which then remain open for other parties to join if they want to participate.

In my discussion with Wendy Cutler and Pascal Lamy, we go on to discuss how strains on global governance and the breakdown of WTO negotiations have led to a "rise of regionalism." Asia in particular has become a locus for new regional multilateral initiatives such as the reformed Comprehensive and Progressive Agreement for Trans-Pacific Partnership (CPTPP) and the Regional Comprehensive Economic Partnership (RCEP).

Deficits of Understanding

The third and perhaps most important gap afflicting global affairs at present is a gap of understanding. Effective communication and mutual understanding are a necessary foundation for all efforts to address our various shared challenges. Yet, it seems we face a serious deficit of mutual understanding right at the time when it is most needed.

Again, there are structural reasons why this gap of understanding has become more serious. On one hand, globalization in its various forms has entwined the fates of different countries and societies more deeply than ever, so it is more important to understand what others are doing and the way they think. On the other hand, while the world has become more complex and interdependent, the stories we tell about it have not evolved and in some ways have become even more simplistic, in part due to trends in politics and communications technology. For example, it is hard to convey the complex reality of a phenomenon like globalization or China's rise in a single tweet or a 15-second TikTok video. In our information-saturated environment, it often seems that the voices heard are those that shout the loudest, shortest, and simplest messages.

Kerry Brown has dedicated much of his academic career to under-standing China. In his most recent book, *China Through European Eyes: 800 Years of Cultural and Intellectual Encounter*, he turns to look at those trying to make sense of China from the outside. In the final dialogue in Part II, Brown identifies several reasons why the gap of under-standing might be more serious when it comes to Western perceptions of China. The first is simply unfamiliarity; for most of history, people in places like the UK and US have had relatively little desire or need to understand places like China. The second problem is something Brown calls "ontological complexity." China is a large, diverse, and complex place that defies easy definition or categorization, and the country has always been something of a hybrid. Historically, Chinese culture and values have been influenced by many different ethical, philosophical, and religious views, forming a flexible worldview that is difficult to label. Economically, China is a hybrid system that combines the domestic private sector, state-owned enterprises, and multinational corporations. Finally, difficulties in understanding China from the outside are compounded by the fact that views of China in the West are often colored by dominant media narratives or psychological factors such as confirmation bias.

PART III: POWER SHIFTS AND GREAT POWER RELATIONS

Relations between China and the US will be central to the story of the twenty-first century. Not only are these two countries the world's two largest economies, they are also the world's two largest trading nations and carbon emitters, as well as being representatives of the developed and developing world, and leading voices for the West and Asia, respectively.

Part III features leading experts from political science, international relations, trade, and business sharing their views on evolving relations between China and the US. Given their outsized role in the world, relations between these two countries will have major consequences, not only for the citizens of both countries, but for the whole world. In particular, whether these two great powers can coexist harmoniously and cooperate will have a large bearing on the future trajectory of the global economy and whether the international community can work together to overcome transnational challenges like climate change and pandemics.

HORIZONTAL AND VERTICAL POWER SHIFTS

The speaker in the first dialogue in Part III is Joseph S. Nye Jr., someone who has spent a distinguished career in academia and government enhancing our understanding of international relations and notions of power. Nye is well known for developing the concept of "soft power," the ability to influence others through attraction rather than coercion or payment. More recently, Nye has turned his focus to how power is changing in the world and how that will affect relations between the US and China.

In the last chapter of his most recent book *Do Morals Matter?* Nye describes two great power shifts occurring in the twenty-first century. The first is the story we are the most familiar with, the "horizontal" power shift from west to east or from Europe and the Atlantic to the Pacific and Asia. To take a rough approximation, in the year 1800, Asia was around half of the world's population and half of the world's economy. By 1900, Asia accounted for half of the world's population but only 20 percent of the world's economy, largely due to the industrial revolution in Europe and North America. Following a rapid resurgence over the last few decades, Asia is now on track to again account for over 50 percent of global GDP by 2040, according to many estimates. While China is central to the rise of Asia, rather than portray the power shift as simply a shift from the US to China, Nye says it is more accurate to say that what we are seeing is the rise of a large group of emerging economies and the formation of a new multipolar world.

As Nye explains, at the same time this horizontal power shift is taking place, there is also a "vertical" power shift underway from governments to non-governmental and transnational actors. It is driven by technology and "ecological globalization"—threats such as climate change and pandemics that don't respect borders and can only be addressed by working with other governments. Nye says that while the horizontal power shift can reconfigure "power over" other countries, the vertical power shift requires a different form of power, called "power with" rather than "power over," because no country can solve transnational problems by itself. Nye stresses that we need to learn to live in a world where both forms of power are managed simultaneously, which is not an easy thing to do.

The Fitzgerald Challenge and the Thucydides Trap

Like Joseph S. Nye Jr., Graham Allison has spent a distinguished career at Harvard and served as a senior official in government. He is the featured speaker in the second dialogue of Part III along with Chen Li, Director of the Center for International Security and Strategy at the School of International Studies, Renmin University of China.

Graham Allison identifies a similar tension to the one Nye describes between horizontal and vertical power shifts when he talks of how leaders of great powers in our age face the "Fitzgerald Challenge." In his 1936 essay, "The Crack-Up," F. Scott Fitzgerald famously writes that the test of a first-class mind is the ability to hold two contradictory ideas in your head at the same time and still function. On one hand, Allison sees fierce competition between the US and China as inevitable because both are determined to be strong in various dimensions such as economics, technology, and diplomacy. At the same time, and somewhat in contradiction with the first idea, unless the US and China can find ways to coordinate and cooperate in dealing with shared threats such as climate, pandemics, and nuclear proliferation, the whole of humanity could be at risk.

Allison is well known for developing the concept of Thucydides's Trap, a deadly pattern of structural stress that results when a rising power challenges a ruling one, as a useful lens to understand China–US relations in our current age. This idea has generated a great deal of discussion as tensions between China and the US have intensified and Allison, Professor Li and I had a fruitful discussion on how to absorb the right lessons from various great power rivalries in history and maintain peace in the twenty-first century.

Think Tank Dialogue on China–US Relations

Amidst ongoing geopolitical tensions, think tanks are well placed to help promote understanding between great powers and explore areas for cooperation through Track II diplomacy. Therefore, CCG was pleased to engage in dialogue with leading US think tanks for the third discussion in Part III. This dialogue features Adam S. Posen from the Peterson Institute for International Economics, J. Stapleton Roy from the Kissinger Institute on China and the United States, John L. Thornton from the Brookings Institution and the Asia Society, as well as Zhu Guangyao and myself representing CCG. These speakers brought a wealth of experience from the fields of economics, finance, diplomacy, and business for a wide-ranging discussion on how to balance competition and cooperation between China and the United States amidst our current global challenges.

The discussion covers structural factors behind current frictions between China and the US, with speakers from both sides noting that while much of the dispute has played out in the field of economics, the driving forces are really political rather than economic. The panel also discussed steps that can be taken to improve China–US relations and potential areas for cooperation such as climate change, the reform of multilateral institutions, and infrastructure. There was a consensus that policymakers need to adopt new mindsets to address twenty-first-century realities and forge new narratives that emphasize shared interests rather than dominance and strategic rivalry.

Another point of agreement was that China and the US need to restore channels for engagement, both at the government and people-to-people level. As John Thornton pointed out, China and the US still enjoy broad and deep ties between universities, NGOs, and individuals. It is crucial to support these exchanges to build societal trust and guard against the drift toward unhelpful policies at the elite level. Hopefully, this is an area where dialogues such as this one between CCG and our counterparts in the US can make some contribution.

MULTIPOLARITY IN THE POST-PANDEMIC ERA

The speaker in the final dialogue in this book is my good friend Kishore Mahbubani, who served as a diplomat for Singapore for over three decades, including stints as Ambassador to the UN and President of the UN Security Council. He is now a Distinguished Fellow at the Asia Research Institute, National University of Singapore. Well versed in the politics and culture of both Asia and the West, Mahbubani is in the rare position of being both extremely well informed and also a neutral third-party observer of China–US relations. The sober analysis and unique perspectives on geopolitics that he shares in our dialogue provide a nice way to cap off this volume.

Summing up the paradox in China–US relations that many speakers highlighted in this series, Mahbubani says that the great geopolitical contest that will be played out between America and China in the coming decades is both "inevitable" and "avoidable." It is "inevitable" because many of the policymakers who will make the tactical decisions that will drive this contest are possessed by a mindset that sees all competition among great powers as a zero-sum game. But the contest is also "avoidable" because fundamentally, there is no contradiction between the core interests of both countries; both would be better off channeling their resources to improve the well-being of their own people and working together to mitigate common threats like climate change, rather than engage in an escalating geopolitical competition that harms not only both countries but also the rest of the world.

In the conclusion to his book *Has China Won?* Mahbubani poses the question: as our only inhabitable planet faces great perils like climate change, should we focus on our differences or our similarities? I would suggest that when we adopt the planetary perspective offered by images like *The Blue Marble* and the *Pale Blue Dot*, the answer is clear.

Note on the Contents of This Book

This book is made up of edited transcripts of discussions that took place between March and October 2021 as part of the CCG Dialogue Series. For this book, they have been arranged thematically as described above rather than presented chronologically. Each transcript has been formalized and edited for readability, brevity, and clarity. Prior to publication, speakers were given the chance to review and edit their transcripts for clarification and accuracy. At the time of recording, each dialogue also featured a short question and answer section at the end. This section has been removed from the edited dialogues due to space considerations and also because the questions raised by reporters often focused on current affairs at the time of recording and tended to have less enduring relevance. It is worth noting that these dialogues were unscripted and free-flowing conversations; the views and opinions expressed by speakers are their own and do not reflect those of their affiliated organizations.

Beijing, China
August 2022

Dr. Henry Huiyao Wang
Dr. Mabel Lu Miao

The Evolution of Globalization

The Year 1000 and the Beginnings of Globalization

A Dialogue Valerie Hansen

Huiyao Wang and Valerie Hansen

On May 27, 2021, CCG hosted a dialogue between CCG President Huiyao Wang and Valerie Hansen, Stanley Woodward Professor of History at Yale University. Hansen is a renowned historian known for her work on China to 1600 and the Silk Road in particular. Her book *The Silk Road: A New History* (2012) tells the story of how this modest commercial artery became the world's most famous cultural superhighway and is one of the most popular books on the topic. In *The Year 1000* (2020), Hansen explores the early beginnings of globalization as people around the world became connected through maritime trade and cultural exchange.

Hansen brought a valuable historical perspective to contemporary issues related to globalization, highlighting lessons from the Song Dynasty, the Silk Road, and other examples from over 1000 years

H. Wang (✉)
Center for China and Globalization (CCG), Beijing, China

V. Hansen
Department of History, Yale University, New Haven, CT, USA

© The Author(s) 2022
H. Wang and L. Miao (eds.), *Understanding Globalization, Global Gaps, and Power Shifts in the 21st Century*,
https://doi.org/10.1007/978-981-19-3846-7_2

ago. Our conversation began with Song Dynasty China, which Hansen describes as the most globalized place on Earth at the time. It goes on to cover topics such as trade and taxation, Confucianism and cultural diffusion, overland trade via the Silk Road, and the key drivers of globalization from the year 1000 up to the present day.

Huiyao Wang: In this dialogue series, we've been talking to many international opinion leaders, well-known scholars, and policymakers about the subject of globalization. You not only study the history of globalization but also are very familiar with China. For example, you have described the port city of Quanzhou, Fujian in the Song Dynasty, which attracted merchants and different kinds of people from different parts of the world. I once visited a museum in Quanzhou where you can see evidence of people visiting from the Middle East, India, and other parts of the world. It's really fascinating to look at that part of history.

What led to this study of globalization? Maybe you can tell us about your background and how you came to these findings about people like the Vikings and traders in Quanzhou, and how they were already moving around the world 1000 years ago.

Valerie Hansen: I came to globalization from the Silk Road. My Silk Road book focused on what is now China and Central Asia. Often, histories of the Silk Road end around the year 1000, as that's when the cave in Dunhuang closes.

There's a theory from a Professor at Peking University named Rong Xinjiang who has proposed that the people living in Dunhuang heard about the fall of Khotan to the armies of the Karakhanids and that their response to that invasion was to close the Document Cave. Not everybody agrees with that theory, but it's a known fact that the Karakhanids did take Khotan before 1006. Another key event around the year 1000 is the Treaty of Chanyuan between the Liao and the Song.

When I was finishing the Silk Road book, I knew about those two events and I knew that the Vikings had touched down in Canada probably around exactly the year 1000, and I wondered if there was any connection among those three events. After five years of looking around, I concluded that a lot of the world was undergoing the same process in the year 1000; regions were getting bigger, people were encountering people from other places and from other regions, and that had a profound effect on people. There are earlier examples of contact between people from different countries. Extensive contact along the Silk Road is one example, and the Roman Empire had trade contacts with India. But in the year 1000, much more of the world was affected by these new contacts, and that's how I ended up with this topic.

Huiyao Wang: In *The Silk Road: A New History*, you describe remarkable findings that have revolutionized our understanding of the trade routes of the Silk Road. In your Silk Road book, you explore eight sites on the road from Xi'an to Samarkand and the Middle East, where envoys, pilgrims, and travelers mix in cosmopolitan communities, and explain how this commercial artery becomes a "cultural superhighway." So, even if we say that globalization starts around the year 1000, maybe the spirit of globalization dates back to the start of the Silk Road. Would you say that the Silk Road also had an impact on globalization?

Valerie Hansen: What's going on in China and Central Asia with the Silk Road has parallels in other parts of the world, like Europe. We know less about Africa and America because we lack written sources from those places.

Regarding the impact, I would say in the period before the year 1000, not that many people were affected. [But of course,] historical processes don't really have a beginning. There's always some earlier trace or evidence of the phenomenon you are researching.

With the Silk Road, there's a shipwreck called Belitung shipwreck, an African or Indonesian boat that was found in the Java Sea off the coast of Indonesia in a place called Belitung. It was carrying Chinese ceramics. The date of the ship is 826–827 and we know that because there's a pot with the date written in Chinese on it. The ship was carrying 60,000 ceramics—that's mass production already in the year 826, and that's the kind of thing I'm talking about in my book, a very early example.

A hundred years later, there's another shipwreck and it's carrying 600,000 Chinese pots on a single ship. So, yes, there's some evidence of [trade contact] earlier [than the year 1000]. But I bring up those two examples because they show how shipping and ocean travel was on a completely different scale than overland trade. The Silk Road in the period before the year 1000 was mostly about overland trade and there was a constraint on overland trade in that animals can carry only so much—there were no machines and no mechanization. I think everyone's mental image of the Silk Road is of camels. In fact, most of the trade, and we know this from Chinese documents, was on horseback or on donkeys or in carts. [Goods are only carried] on camels when you're going through the desert on sand and if people have a choice, they avoid sand and go on roads.

I think there's a real change in the year 1000 because we see this shift to sea travel. People travel on the sea a little bit before 1000, but in the year 1000—in different places with the Vikings, the Polynesians, and the Chinese—we see the beginnings of genuinely long-distance sea travel.

Huiyao Wang: That's a very interesting comparison. What do you think of the different phases of globalization? Trade is one element, but there is also religious and cultural exchange. For example, Xuanzang went to India.[1] In the Tang Dynasty, Japanese students came to China. So, what do you think about the different phases of globalization?

Valerie Hansen: It's funny, I was actually going to ask you the same question about the phases of globalization. Let me start now and go back in time. The consensus among historians is that the current phase of globalization started around the 1970s–1980s. A key thing that observers look at is "space–time compression." If you can get on an airplane and travel from New York to Beijing in a day, space and time have been compressed. A journey which by boat could take months is suddenly reduced to one day. This [space–time compression] is a hallmark of the phase of globalization we're living in now. Airplanes, computers, even the fact that you and I can have this conversation and see each other in real-time—these are new things that did not exist in the past. I'd say that's the current phase which starts around the 1970s, do you agree?

Huiyao Wang: Yes, I think that you're right. As we discussed, I think there are some early sparks of globalization during the Silk Road. By the year 1000, people really start to move around the world and globalization picks up momentum.

Later, we have Columbus reaching the Americas and Zheng He, the Chinese mariner, who led seven expeditions to Southeast Asia or even as far as Africa. Things started to move around—products, seeds, or even disease. But I would say that globalization has really accelerated since the Industrial Revolution. Technology has sped up globalization to the point where today we are connected in real-time. But looking back at history, I think it's fascinating to try to trace the origins of these trends.

So, let's go back to history. Over 1000 years ago, when Quanzhou welcomed so many foreign merchants and travelers, Confucianism was

---

[1] Xuanzang (602–664), Buddhist monk and scholar who traveled to India and translated Buddhist scriptures from Sanskrit into Chinese.

already prevalent in China. What do you think of Confucianism and its impact on the Song dynasty? Also, from a historical perspective, how did globalization impact China? You write in your book that at the time, China already had a population of around 100 million people, when the global population was probably only around 250 million, meaning that China accounted for 35–40 percent of the global population. Maybe you can describe the Song Dynasty and the historical impact of globalization, which were covered in your book.

Valerie Hansen: In the book, I say that Song Dynasty China was the most globalized place on Earth at the time. The reason I say that is that so many people in China lived on the coast, as is still true today, and people on the coast of China are much more affected by these international trends than people in the interior. Quanzhou is a very good example of a coastal city that was affected by globalization. As you said, you can see in the museum the evidence of foreign residents. There were many tombstones of people in Arabic. There were also a lot of Indians in Quanzhou, and you can see their presence in stones from preserved pieces of Hindu temples, which are no longer standing today.

The reason China was so important was that it was already a manufacturing center. There were huge workshops and kilns making ceramics. I mentioned the ceramics from the shipwrecks because they are the thing that survive, archaeologically. But we know that the Song Dynasty also exported metals, not only metal objects like pots, knives, and weapons, but also bars of iron, lead, and tin.

China had massive exports carried on Chinese ships and used the compass so ships could navigate. What people less often think about are Chinese imports and how many things they were bringing in. As I talked about in the book, in Quanzhou, lots of people wanted *xiang*, which is a broad term covering fragrant woods like sandalwood, and aloeswood. In the Song, people were bringing in these fragrant woods, they were bringing in foods, spices, and other natural products from Southeast Asia and the Arabian Peninsula. There was a huge demand in China for these foreign goods and that's what was fueling the trade.

You asked me about the Confucians. The Confucians didn't say that much about this trade. There's an American historian named Charles Hartman who has just brought out a new book about the history of the Song. One of his arguments is that there were two groups within the Chinese government. There's a famous group we know about because they became Confucian thinkers. There was also a less famous group of technocrats, a lot of whom were linked to the likes of Wang Anshi.[2]

These technocrats were looking at governance and figuring out the best way to tax trade, which is one of the interesting innovations of the Song period. Everyone knows about the tribute system which existed in the Tang, and it existed in the Song, but it somewhat falls to the side as the government was spending much more of its energy on taxing ships that arrived in Chinese ports. They collected three kinds of taxes and there were only certain ports that had the bureaucracy to do this kind of taxation.

I talked about Quanzhou and how they handled this before they were recognized as a city that could do this kind of taxation. In certain ports, the ship pulled into the port, the government officials got on the boat, and then they just took a fixed percentage of the ships' cargo, which changes during the Song Dynasty. Then the officials looked at what was left, and said: "Oh, these are the goods we have a government monopoly on." There were very sophisticated ideas about which goods should be sold by a monopoly and they confiscated a share of those. Then there was another category of goods called "coarse goods," which officials cared less about, so they were taxed but the ship could sell them in the port. When you look at Song Dynasty documents, you can see that officials were trying to decide how much they could tax; too much, and the merchants won't come again. If they taxed too little, then the government doesn't have the revenues it needs. It was very sophisticated, and I don't know of anything like that happening in other parts of the world in the year 1000.

Huiyao Wang: It's fascinating to hear you talk about the vivid life of the Song Dynasty and how it was the most globalized place in the world at that time. Actually, my father was from Hangzhou, and I see how the region has been revived in today's China, drawing on strong traditions from that period. And Quanzhou, as you've mentioned, had already become one of the biggest ports in China, and probably in the world, too.

So, are there any lessons we can learn from the Song Dynasty and how they were able to become so globalized, with an advanced tax system that was well balanced so as to not drive merchants away, but rather motivate them to do more foreign trade?

---

[2] Wang Anshi (1021–1086), an economist, philosopher, poet, and politician during the Song dynasty.

Also, the Song Dynasty signed the Chanyuan Treaty with the Liao, which managed to secure a long period of peace and security. Graham Allison also mentioned this treaty in my talk with him as an exception that might show a way to avoid the Thucydides Trap.

So, what lessons can we learn from the Song Dynasty for our current times? We mentioned ports and China now has seven out of the world's ten largest ports. In some ways, it is like China is trying to revive the glory days of the Song regarding trade and globalization. But China also faces a lot of challenges, as does globalization itself. Comparing globalization now and then, what are the similarities and what are the new challenges?

Valerie Hansen: These are interesting questions. My book cites the year 1000 as a beginning of globalization, but I'm not claiming globalization was fully developed at that time. There were probably just a handful of geographers writing in Arabic who had a mental vision of the whole globe and knew which parts of the globe had people on them. They didn't know about the Americas, but they knew how big the globe was and they knew how many of those places people were living in. I think a big difference between globalization in the year 1000 up to 1500 and today, is that in the period I'm writing about, there were natural limits on globalization. I mentioned the shipwreck from the year 930 that had 600,000 ceramics on it. The reason we know about that ship is that it sank in the Java Sea. So, historically it was possible for an exporting country to export a certain amount of goods, but never enough to overwhelm local production.

Archaeologists have found Chinese ceramics all along the coast of Southeast Asia, India, the Middle East, and East Africa. You talked about Zheng He's route. The Chinese were active, and much earlier than Zheng He, on this route all the way from Guangzhou and Quanzhou to Mombasa in East Africa. We know Chinese goods were being sold all along that route, but we also know that local manufacturers were continuing to produce because archaeologically we can see copies of Chinese vessels. There's a picture in my book of a Chinese vessel that was found in a city in Iran called Shush, or historically Susa. And we also have a local copy, which was actually inferior. The Chinese vessel is quite beautiful and has a clean, white glaze. The local vessel has a kind of a bad glaze with cracks in it. So, we know that local manufacturing continued. I think that is one of the big changes from today. Because of [transport technology like] large cargo airplanes, one country can produce so much that it can take over the whole market of another country. I think that's one of the things that we have to think about going forward with globalization. And I think that the pandemic has shown us that being entirely dependent on another country for any product is probably not a good long-term strategy.

Huiyao Wang: I agree. Another lesson we can take is that the Song Dynasty flourished in part because they secured a relatively long period of peace through the Chanyuan Treaty. So, for globalization to deepen and generate prosperity, peace is important. Another lesson is that trade can bond and link people together, as business interests serve as a common denominator to unite people. Reading your book, we find there are so many interesting lessons from history.

As a historian, what do you think about the impact of Confucianism? Confucianism has had a great influence on the region through a kind of "cultural globalization." In the Tang Dynasty, Japanese students came to Chang'an. Confucianism also had an impact on neighboring countries like Vietnam. What do you think about regionalization in Asia, in which Confucianism can play some role? I think that Confucius still has a big influence in Greater China and other parts of Asia.

Valerie Hansen: I think one of the things that's very interesting about the year 1000 is you can see certain regions taking shape. Actually, you can see that earlier in the case of East Asia. I would say that was a very good example of China's soft power.

People in what's now modern Korea, modern Japan, and modern Vietnam all adopted the Chinese writing system, and there was a [regional] book market. Books were destroyed when Kaifeng fell to the Jurchens. The Imperial Library was damaged and a lot of books were lost, but they can be recovered because there are copies available on the Korean Peninsula and in Japan. So, there are very clear links among East Asian countries using Chinese characters. It means that texts can move and don't have to be translated. In a period when translation was so slow and expensive, to be able to leave texts in their original language was very valuable.

One of the interesting things about regions is that they can change. So, we can look and say, there's the region of "East Asia"—China, Japan, Korea, and Vietnam, and they have similarities. But if you go back to the year 1000, one of the things that's interesting about the Song was that it was a very economically prosperous dynasty, but geographically a small dynasty. The Song ceded the 16 prefectures to the Liao and when the Jin Dynasty invaded, all of northern China came under foreign rule. So, you could draw the regions in East Asia a little bit differently, which I try to do in the book.

The region of territory under the Liao and the Jin had much more contact with Japan and Korea than the Song territory. There was an idea that the world was going to come to an end in 1052.[3] That idea did not circulate in Song, but it did circulate among the Liao, in Japan, and in Korea. So, I think one of the things that we can see is that a country may belong to more than one region. When we draw a region, we tend to think that some countries belong to this region and other countries belong to that region. But when we look at how people in the past lived, at one moment they may see themselves as part of one region, in another moment, they may see themselves as part of another region.

Huiyao Wang: It's very interesting to hear that in the year 1000, East Asia was taking some kind of shape. Chinese characters were being used in Japan, Korea, and even Vietnam. It seems Chinese characters and probably Confucianism play some role in the forming of this region, and we still see the influence of this today. For example, East Asian culture emphasizes respect for seniority, education, and hard work.

In the course of its history, China has generally been relatively peaceful and neutral. For example, even during Zheng He's seven expeditions, they never conquered or colonized any place. That's interesting to see.

Valerie Hansen: If you allow me, I will disagree with you about Zheng He. Most of the time it was peaceful, but there were times when the Chinese intervened in succession disputes in countries. Nowadays in China, Zheng He is often described as a very peaceful explorer. But when you look at sources from the time, while it was usually peaceful trade, it was a huge shock to many places to have so many people arrive on those ships. Zheng He's fleet, which at its fullest had 28,000 people, was arriving in places that may not have had enough food for that many people. We also have historic evidence of cases, for example, when a King who was loyal and had sent tribute mission to China would die, a son takes over, and the Chinese don't approve of that son and then they intervene. So, I would say "mostly" peaceful for Zheng He.

Huiyao Wang: But at least they didn't really conquer any place and stay there forever. That was even 100 years before Columbus. So, at least it was largely peaceful.

---

[3] In some Buddhist circles at the time there was a belief that the world come to an end when the Final Dharma era began, which some Buddhists believed was the year 1052.

Maybe now we can talk a bit about contemporary globalization. We have already had a thousand years of globalization. As a historian, how do you see the future of globalization and what are the challenges and opportunities? What are some issues we should look at, such as technology, people, migration, trade, or the digital economy?

Valerie Hansen: Well, I'm convinced that globalization began in the year 1000 on a worldwide basis and that it's here to stay. I think it's part of the human condition. The motivation for globalization is that people want new things. Sometimes it's new ideas, but often it's particular commodities.

In my book, I write about how when the Vikings arrived in what is now Canada, they met the local people, the indigenous peoples of Canada. The two groups looked at each other. This phenomenon happened in lots of different places. They look at each other and think, what do those people have that we don't have? They looked at the Vikings and said, you have this red cloth. We don't have that red cloth, which is something we want. The Vikings looked at them, and they said, oh, you have these fabulous furs from animals that we've never seen; we want those. Then, they begin to trade, which makes me think that human impulse underlies globalization—a thousand years ago and today too. The same thing as how people go into a store and see something they've never seen before and think "I have to have that." That's also true in Quanzhou in the year 1000—"the fragrant wood from Southeast Asia is so wonderful, I'm going to build a whole room out of this wood, it's that important to me." That's something we can see.

The motivation for globalization starts very early, and it's on an individual basis, which is that people desire these new things. But we can also see very early on that some people were affected adversely by this trade. When I was researching the book, I was very interested in anti-globalization riots, such as those that took place in Cairo in 996 and in Constantinople in the early 1180s. These were reactions against foreign merchants, where you have local people saying, "oh, these people are just so much richer than our local merchants. They live in nicer houses, they've taken our women as their wives." So, from the very beginning of globalization, we can see some people benefiting from globalization, but we can also see people who are actively harmed by it, who object to it, and want to control it.

Thinking about the future of globalization, I think the question is how we can control these forces. In the modern world, maybe we should take advantage of globalization, but make sure that people who have lost their jobs because of globalization have some protection. I think the issue for us going forward is figuring out ways for governments to cooperate to lessen the negative impact of globalization. You and Tom Friedman talked about how the United Nations is maybe not strong enough to do this. I don't know, because I'm a historian and not good at looking into the future, you're better at that than I am. Do you see any avenues forward for greater cooperation among different governments or different places?

Huiyao Wang: I think you've given an excellent analysis. I also believe that early globalization was motivated by trade and exchanging products. But as you said, while globalization has generated a lot of wealth, there are also widening gaps within and between societies. Today, we see the gap between rich and poor is getting wider and wider, even during the pandemic. When I talked to Martin Wolf of the *Financial Times*, he emphasized how globalization is global, but democracy is local. Local citizens have only limited control over the global movement of goods, talent, and capital. Tom Friedman is right, we need global governance, but we do not have a true "global government" yet, so I think we have to strengthen multilateralism, rather than reverting to unilateralism and fighting against each other.

Reviewing the history of globalization, when globalization was just starting, it was manageable and its impact was limited. But once it gets into full swing, globalization affects everyone's lives, so governments need to consider how to forge a more inclusive and equal form of globalization.

We need to strengthen the UN and the multilateral system. We may also have to invent some new multilateral governance institutions. For example, figuring out how to tax the activities of multinational corporations in a way that is fair for both the home and host country. Also, finding ways to dismantle barriers and to restrain nationalism. The Internet transcends borders, but if there is too much nationalism and populism, that could work against globalization. I think our discussion today is significant because in looking back to the origins and successes of globalization, we can draw lessons for how to address the current challenges facing globalization.

Moving on to your book *The Silk Road: A New History*, which has become famous. According to your account, the development of the Silk Road was influenced by economic conditions. There was a lack of infrastructure and it was difficult to travel long distances across land, which limited the development of globalization.

Nowadays, we have lots more infrastructure. China has developed infrastructure quickly over the last four decades and started the Belt and Road Initiative. Since World War II, we have had a trade boom and economic booms. Could we next have an "infrastructure revolution," a modern infrastructure-supported Silk Road? The Belt and Road takes inspiration from the historical Silk Road and other routes like the Spice trade routes. These could be combined to support a more multilateral global trend for the future.

Valerie Hansen: I share the positive spirit, but as a Silk Road historian, it's important to remember that when we talk about the period of the Silk Road, the Chinese also had a military presence in Central Asia. The reason there was so much silk moving is that the Tang Dynasty had a chronic shortage of coins. The Tang had three kinds of currencies: grain in fixed measures, coins (which there were not enough of), and silks. Silk doesn't seem like a very good currency today, but it was pretty good at that time because it held its value and in some cases was lighter than the coins. That's important because with the Silk Road the constraint was the difficulty of carrying things over land. You're right that modern infrastructure makes things different. There was nothing comparable to current high-speed trains and highways in those days.

When we think about the Silk Road, there are periods when the Chinese had a strong military presence in Central Asia. After 755, after the An Lushan Rebellion, there are periods where the Chinese were much less present in Central Asia. Those periods may be the ones that tell us the most about the possibilities for multilateralism, when we can see political units of roughly the same size cooperating. For example, the rulers of Dunhuang and the rulers of Khotan had a lot of exchange. Neither of them was a giant state in the way that the Tang dynasty was.

There aren't that many examples from the past of giant states successfully cooperating with smaller states. When we talk about the Treaty of Chanyuan, that's important because the Chinese made some concessions to the Liao and the peace lasts for 100 years. But while the Song were not fighting with the Liao, they were fighting with the Tanguts (Western Xia). There was constant war, so the Song did not achieve their goal of perfect peace. Therefore, I would say that things are complicated. Things are complex now, and things were complex in the past.

Huiyao Wang: You describe how marine globalization starts to get going around the year 1000. Now, we are in an era where overland or continental globalization is possible because of infrastructure. For example, last year, intercontinental trade between China and Europe increased 50 percent, with a cohort of trains moving back and forth.

I want to ask another question about globalization during the Song dynasty, when China was possibly the most globalized place in the world. As we are talking about 1000 years of globalization, and the Song is a prime reflection of this process, maybe you can talk a bit more about globalization during the Song dynasty.

Valerie Hansen: To me, one of the hallmarks of globalization is that people produce something and can't even see where their goods go. I think that's why people have this feeling today of things being out of control; they make something and they don't know where it's going or who is buying it.

In the Song, we see massive production of ceramics, as well as mining and textiles. These products leave China and travel to Southeast Asia, India, the Middle East, and Africa. People in China don't know that much about where those things are going. The same thing is true of the people they are trading with, those trading natural products coming from Southeast Asia. We have descriptions of forest-dwelling peoples who lived basically by hunting and gathering suddenly having to produce (hunt and gather) for a foreign market, for example, Kingfisher birds with blue feathers, an import highly valued by the Chinese. Imagine somebody living in a forest in Indonesia, collecting and hunting these birds, and then bringing them to some broker.

In the modern world, because of the freer movement of information, we can learn more about distant markets. But distant markets still have a large impact; one year you might sell a huge amount of a good, but the next year the market collapses, and people lose their jobs and you don't know why. I think that it is worth thinking about—how we can harness information to mitigate this damage of globalization in the future.

Huiyao Wang: I think that one of the characteristics of the Song and Tang is that China was quite open. Buddhism, Christianity, and Islam came to China. These foreign religions and cultures contributed to the opening-up and development of China. This historical experience suggests that China should continue to be open and inclusive, welcome different cultures, and promote mutual learning between different places. The Song and Tang dynasties were able to coexist peacefully with the other parts of the world. Confucianism also established a strong foothold during the Song Dynasty. All of these elements probably played some role in promoting globalization during the Song Dynasty.

Valerie Hansen: I think that's true. I find the free exchange of information, especially in this early period, quite inspiring. There's a person I talk about in the book named al-Biruni. He's an advisor to a ruler, based in Afghanistan but also spent time in India. Some envoys came from the Liao to visit his ruler. He has a chance to talk to them and to learn about North China. He learns a lot about South China too. He writes about China in Arabic and he writes about the encounter between his ruler and the envoy from the Liao dynasty. Unfortunately, the Liao sent an envoy in 1026 or 1027, and they want to initiate diplomatic relations, but the ruler says no. I think we should not take any lessons from that because it's an example of closed-mindedness. But his advisor al-Biruni talks to the envoys from the Liao dynasty and uses the chance to learn more about China. I think it is important to learn from other countries and from people in those other countries about how those societies function.

Huiyao Wang: We've reviewed the history of globalization and you have proposed that in a way, globalization started in the year 1000, which is almost 500 years before Columbus went to America. You also talked about how the Song dynasty was one of the most globalized places in the world in the year 1000.

I think it's important to learn from history and draw on the spirit of globalization as we face new challenges in the current day, like deglobalization, populism, and nationalism. Revisiting history can help us to find new solutions, such as how to address inequality and promote openness. It has been a great discussion and I really appreciate you giving your time. Maybe you could say a few words to conclude as a final remark.

Valerie Hansen: As you were talking, I was thinking about how in the beginning of globalization, the forces of globalization were much weaker than they are now. But we can already see that they adversely affected some people, so much that they kill some foreign merchants who are living in Cairo and in Constantinople. There's also the Huang Chao rebellion when there's a massacre of Arab merchants who are living in Guangzhou. The death toll is debated. But many people died in these riots.

In my view, the forces of globalization were weaker around the year 1000 and the checks on globalization were stronger than they are now—like the risks involved in shipping and the high number of shipwrecks, the costs of overland trade which meant that there just wasn't that much trade going over land, because it cost so much, camel caravans could get lost, and people could die if they were robbed.

I think as we go forward, we have to think about what kinds of checks we may need to institute to try to balance the impact of globalization. The pandemic, in a way, is a check on the process of globalization. We've had over a year to think very hard about this world we live in and how we're going to go forward in the future. And I think you're going to have to find a futurologist, not a historian, to tell you about that.

Huiyao Wang: I think that globalization is very resilient, full of vitality and its own momentum. There will be setbacks and zigzags, but the trend will continue.

As you said, initially, globalization did not touch that many people, but today we have 200 million Chinese people learning English and 150 million Chinese people going abroad for tourism each year. Globalization is here to stay and we have to learn to live with each other peacefully. That's a lesson we must learn from the history of globalization. So once again, thank you very much and I hope when you come to China, we will see you again and invite you to visit CCG. Thank you very much, Professor Hansen, it was nice talking to you.

Valerie Hansen: Thank you so much. I really appreciate you taking the time to have such a dialogue. It was really a pleasure.

Transformations in the Global Economy

A Dialogue with Martin Wolf

Huiyao Wang and Martin Wolf

On May 12, 2021, CCG hosted a dialogue between CCG President Huiyao Wang and Martin Wolf, Chief Economics Commentator at the *Financial Times*. Wolf has had an illustrious career in journalism and is considered a leading authority on globalization. He previously worked at the World Bank and has been covering the world economy and global finance for the *Financial Times* since 1987. He is also the author of several influential books, including *Why Globalization Works* (2004), *Fixing Global Finance* (2008), and *The Shifts and the Shocks: What We've Learned—And Have Still to Learn—From the Financial Crisis* (2014). His forthcoming book deals with the crisis facing democratic capitalism.

A sought-after speaker on the global circuit, Wolf is a regular participant in the annual China Development Forum, where I have met him several times over the years, as well as at other events around the world. This conversation took place in May 2021, at a time when the global

H. Wang (✉)
Center for China and Globalization (CCG), Beijing, China

M. Wolf
Financial Times, London, UK

H. Wang and L. Miao (eds.), *Understanding Globalization,
Global Gaps, and Power Shifts in the 21st Century*,
https://doi.org/10.1007/978-981-19-3846-7_3

economy had begun its gradual recovery from the worst of the pandemic-induced global recession but still faced many challenges and uncertainties ahead. Our discussion covered a wide range of topics, from the economic impact of COVID-19 and the measures being taken to support the global recovery, to challenges facing global governance, whether China and the US can overcome their differences to reinvigorate multilateralism, and the evolving nature of globalization in the post-pandemic era.

Huiyao Wang: Good Morning, Martin, great to have you, and maybe you can say a few words to our audience to start.

Martin Wolf: I'm very pleased to have this dialogue on a crucial subject at a crucial time. We are going through extraordinary transformations in the world order because of economic developments, because of political developments, and of course, because of the pandemic. So, we are all being forced to rethink our view of the world and how it's going to evolve. I'm just completing a book on the future of the West. But I have come to the view that this decade is looking increasingly like what one might call a "hinge of history," one of those decisive moments in human affairs that will determine the future of our world for a long time. Will it be prosperous and peaceful? Will we manage our big challenges, above all, climate? Will we manage to cooperate satisfactorily or will the order we have created in the last 20 or 30 years—the order of global cooperation, and for all its failures, globalization—collapse?

I think those issues are very much alive and the next 10 years or so is likely to provide us with answers. I am very concerned about the developments we see. I've been around for a long time and I think this is possibly the most challenging period of my lifetime. I was born immediately after the Second World War, so I didn't experience that catastrophe. But I've been alive now for 75 years and this is a very challenging period we're now entering. The pandemic spurred technological advances but also intensified inequality and debt.

Huiyao Wang: Thanks, Martin. I agree with you, the current challenges we are facing are unprecedented. The pandemic has swept the world and the global economy is struggling to catch up. So, 2021 is to be a year of recovery. Maybe you could share a bit of your outlook. Is this pandemic crisis going to reshape the global economy, the political landscape, or the way global governance is conducted?

Martin Wolf: There's so much to say, I'll try and keep it brief. So, the first point is the one you noted; we've now had two very significant global crises in less than fifteen years. The last one was the financial crisis of 2007–2009, but it went on in Europe to 2015, so it was a long crisis. Just a few years later we were hit by the pandemic—an event that many had predicted, indeed it's not at all surprising. Humanity has a long history of experiencing pandemics. Nevertheless, we didn't know when the next one would happen, and then it happened, and that's been another huge shock. In a way, it's been the most global economic crisis there has ever been, in the sense that it has affected basically every country in the world more profoundly than any other comparable event, at least in modern times. When I think of modern times, I mean since the Industrial Revolution, so about the last two centuries or so. Of course, there have been much more damaging pandemics in the past, such as the Black Death in the fourteenth century, but that was so long ago that the memories of it have largely gone, except in the history books.

If we think of the pandemic, it was global, it was sudden, and it led to a very sharp contraction last year, particularly in the first half of last year, across a very large range of economies—particularly in the West, but also a bit earlier in China. What can we say about its social and economic effects? I think we can say the following things: the first, which in a way is the most interesting and important, is how big the economic damage was of a pandemic that—at least in terms of its fatalities—was historically relatively minor. I've been looking at the famous Spanish Flu of 1918, so just over 100 years ago. Nobody knows exactly how many people died then, but the central estimate is about 50 million, which given population growth, would be equivalent to 200 million now. So far, this pandemic has killed fewer than three million. So, it's a much smaller pandemic in its health effects, but its economic effects have been much bigger, so far as we know. Of course, [a hundred years ago] we didn't measure economies in the way we do today, but [the economic impact of the current pandemic is] still much bigger.

Why is that? The important point is that our societies, and I think this is a very good thing, put an enormous value on human life, and we are prepared to pay an enormous economic price to protect human lives. That was clear in China, where you closed down Wuhan, for example, in order to contain the virus, regardless of the cost. The same was true across the Western world, we basically closed down our economies and people stayed at home. Even in relatively poor countries there were lockdowns. So, we really care about human life, that's the first big lesson and I think that's fantastic.

The second thing we learned is that we have the means to do something about [the pandemic] because our technology has advanced so much. We have learned, as we're now experiencing with this Zoom call, that we can now run much of our modern economy without physically meeting. That generates huge inequality in our societies because the people who can [work remotely] tend to be the more prosperous and have graduate degrees. With the great exception of the medical profession, by and large, people with degrees have been pretty safe. But people who must work face-to-face with other people have not [been safe] and that is creating huge social divisions as a result of the pandemic, and also great divergence among countries because some countries with more advanced economies are able to do much more online than others. That's the inequality point we've learned, which is very important.

The third thing we've learned is about the immense advances in medical science and our ability, which nobody would have really believed a year ago, to create billions of vaccines, which work, and distribute them, [albeit] very unevenly and very unequally across the world. This is also an extraordinary lesson.

So, what does this mean? And this is my last point for the immediate future. The countries that have controlled the disease successfully— notably China, but also South Korea, Australia, and New Zealand—have reopened [their economies] pretty well. Economies that have managed mass vaccination programs like the US, and now the UK, and over the next few months Europe, will also expand very rapidly. I expect a big global recovery this year and next year, led by the big economies—basically, the big Western economies and advanced Asian economies like China, which together account for about 75–80 percent of the world economy. Unfortunately, there are lots of other countries which are in a much worse situation. They don't have the vaccines yet and they're very dependent on tourists, who are still not going to travel. They have some very big problems. Look at South America, India, or Africa.

Then there's the final thing—the remnant of the crisis, which is a huge amount of debt, a lot of dollar debt. That's going to be perfectly manageable, in my view, in the developed countries. But it will be much more problematic in emerging countries. So, we will emerge [from the pandemic] strongly but very unequally. Lastly, the crisis has generated a lot of ill will, political instability, and anger that will affect the shape of international relations in the future.

Huiyao Wang: Thank you for a very timely and broad analysis of the global pandemic situation. I think you're right, we'll see a recovery, but it won't be smooth and linear—there will be zigzags and ups and downs.

Martin, you are something of a guru on globalization and in 2004 published the book *Why Globalization Works*. Over the last 100 years, globalization has generated enormous prosperity but has also now brought unprecedented challenges. Amidst the pandemic and complications over vaccines, more countries seem to have become susceptible to populism and nationalism. Many countries have closed borders or adopted protectionist measures. How do you see the future of globalization? Will it continue, can it be adjusted? Can we forge a more inclusive globalization, as you've often suggested?

Martin Wolf: Another very big question. When I analyzed globalization in *Why Globalization Works* nearly 20 years ago, [that book] was a defense of globalization. At that time, there were a lot of critics [of globalization] in the West. People were saying that globalization is very bad for developing countries, it's exploitative and we should stop it. I said, well, actually the evidence is very clear: [globalization] is good for developing countries, with China the foremost example. China's incredible growth couldn't have happened without Reform and Opening-up.

In *Why Globalization Works*, I said there are two drivers: technology and policy. They do interact a bit, as in the long-run, technology is influenced by policy. But in the medium-run, [the drivers are basically] technology and policy. So, let's look at where we are on technology and policy.

Technology is the underlying potential for globalization, given technological realities, and policy is what governments allow. On technology, one possibility has been to a substantial extent exhausted, quite naturally. That is the unbundling of supply chains across the world. This has been going for quite a long time—we had pretty clear evidence that 10–12 years ago after the financial crisis, [globalization in terms of supply chain unbundling] was slowing.

I think the reason it was slowing was that a large part of the opportunities to unbundle physical supply chains had already been exploited. Some supply chains that had been unbundled [in which China played a role] were actually moving into China, thus becoming "Chinese" supply chains. In addition, the enormous cost advantages that countries like China and Vietnam had in the 1980s and 1990s were diminishing because of a wonderful thing—wages were going up. The result was a completely natural slowing of the unbundling of physical supply chains. This won't reverse until there are huge new technological improvements.

The globalizing potential of links such as transport, the Internet and telecommunications are [no longer] being transformed, with one exception we will come to in a moment. To give you an example, airplanes move basically about as fast now as they did 40 years ago. We've got huge container ships, but they are probably now about as big as they are ever going to get. Look what just happened in the Suez Canal [which was blocked by a ship in March 2021]. The shipping container was a great invention but it is now roughly 70 years old. Technologically, the unbundling of supply chains and the movement of goods may well have reached a natural plateau, relative to our economy.

But there's another completely different potential, which is what I think of as "virtual globalization" or the globalization of ideas, broadly defined. We've discovered in this crisis that it's possible to operate highly interactively without being in the same place. That will generate huge potential for interaction among human beings—economic interaction, cultural interaction, and interaction in terms of ideas. Here, the relevant divisions are linguistic more than anything else, and with advances in AI, even those will diminish. I'm sure we will soon be in a world in which I can talk in English to someone in China speaking in Mandarin, and we will both hear perfect translations by AI and be able to have a conversation. That may not be this decade, maybe the decade after, but I think this will happen. So, I think virtual globalization has tremendous potential. That is a wonderful thing. It will be very difficult to isolate yourself from the world, intellectually and culturally, something I'm in favor of, but it will also create some challenges.

Then there's policy. Here, it's pretty clear: we have become more suspicious of one another and that's partly because of divergent political developments. I'm not going to talk about China, but I think this is pretty clear in that country. In the West, our societies have become more divided; that was happening before the financial crisis, but the financial crisis and now the pandemic have made it even more so. It's made people more suspicious of one another and politics more populist and more deeply divided. And when people don't really like one another in a country, the one thing they can often agree on, and this is age-old, is that they dislike foreigners even more. I'm afraid xenophobia could be the thing that brings people together. That could be true even in China and certainly in the West. As that's happening, politicians may say, "It's nothing to do with what's going on in our country. It's all *their* fault", as when Mr. Trump said, "It's all the fault of the Chinese." People will listen to this and we see this happening, not to the same degree in Europe, but it's happening. That's the first thing.

Then, we are in the midst of a massive power shift. Let's be completely realistic about it: the Europeans and their colonial offshoot, the US, have been used to running the world for hundreds of years. They don't like to see this changing and they don't know what to do about it. I think it's also true that China has not yet worked out what it wants to do about its new position. This is creating tremendous political tensions—how do we "run the world" when we no longer [actually] run it?

This situation is creating more ill will and leading to a desire to protect themselves and make themselves more secure by reducing reliance on others and by making sure that they remain a world leader in technologies. This is all quite understandable, but from a policy view, it tends to work against globalization. You saw that in the trade war that Mr. Trump launched against China. You can see that in frictions in international relations and suspicion of one another that comes out in rhetoric on both sides, particularly in the US. This affects globalization because American companies then say, it looks like my government doesn't want me to be involved in China and if I must choose, as an American company, I've got to do what my government wants. I think the globalization of goods and of supply chains is going to go into reverse, creating regional supply chains, whether they be Chinese- or Western-dominated. Then we have this overlay of the future of "virtual globalization" which is reinforced by one of the greatest technological developments of our era—Artificial Intelligence. So overall, it's a very complex and very difficult and uncertain picture.

Huiyao Wang: I'm interested in your upcoming book, *The Crisis of Democratic Capitalism*. We see a huge wealth gap between the richest in society and the rest of the population. In a way, China has become a scapegoat for this kind of inequality, while multinationals reap large profits around the world but bring only limited benefits to their host and home countries. Has global governance fallen behind in areas such as ensuring multinationals do their fair share? I notice that recently President Biden has been discussing how to increase the wages of the lowest-paid workers and also proposed a global flat tax rate. Also, even during the pandemic, we have seen the top 1 percent become richer as Wall Street hits record highs. What is your take on these issues?

Martin Wolf: The questions you pose are very deep ones. Let's start with the inequality issue. The statistics, such as they are, suggest that there's a pretty high level of inequality in China, too. The big difference is that given the immense rate of growth in China, pretty much everybody in China has benefited substantially from growth, so rising inequality matters less.

In the West, particularly in America, rising inequality has coincided with pretty flat real income growth for a very large part of the population and particularly the bottom half, though this is a pretty complex and controversial topic and I won't be able to go into all the statistics. The reason for that is you've got rising inequality of wealth and income when overall productivity growth has been fairly slow. In China, productivity growth has been shooting ahead at 6–8 percent a year for decades, until relatively recently, as it has slowed since 2012.

In the West, productivity growth has been much slower. One reason is that countries like the US are already relatively advanced so they can't gain much from importing new technology from elsewhere. They have to develop within themselves. Also, I believe that given the structure of our economy—basically, the increasing domination of personal services which are difficult to automate—it's more difficult to increase productivity than it used to be. I think that in the next 20 years, China will begin to suffer from the same problem as industry becomes a diminishing force in the economy, as industry is always one of the sectors where productivity growth is fastest. After that, you are left with the other activities—such as hospitals, schools, or looking after old people—where it's really hard to raise productivity. So, you end up with an economy with a huge service sector, a lot of which is quite stagnant, productivity-wise. That may change in the future, but that's where we are now.

So, productivity growth has been slow in the West and inequality has been rising. Logically, that means a large proportion of the population haven't seen rising incomes, which causes anger. In societies with very diverse populations, this has created interethnic friction, allowing politicians to play on a kind of ethnic cultural war as part of their political strategy, what I think of as "blaming the other," both internally and also externally—because the other "other" you can blame are foreigners. The characteristic of right-wing populism which has become so powerful is that you blame domestic "others" and foreign "others" for what's gone wrong. That's what Donald Trump represented and it's what the Republicans now represent. You can see similar things, though not to the same degree, in Europe—in Britain, Italy, and France, much less in Germany, but it's there.

This has a second huge consequence—the return of nationalism. I would like to suggest there is a fundamental moral underpinning to this, which brings us to a deep conceptual fact related to your question. The capitalist economy tends to be a global economy. This was true in the nineteenth century and Karl Marx wrote very well on this. The reason for this is very simple. If you are a capitalist, you are in the market and there are opportunities globally, huge opportunities. That's why Chinese entrepreneurs have gone global and why American entrepreneurs went global and all the rest of it. So, the world capitalist economy is naturally cosmopolitan. That was Marx's great insight. It's a cosmopolitan system, which in many ways is a good thing, and it's an effective system for developing growth.

But as the economy becomes more global, national control over the economy shrinks inevitably. Because the economy is more global, it's not all under your control in the way it used to be. Whatever the political system is, government is national, not global. International government essentially rests on the voluntary cooperation of national governments, which have domestic legitimacy and domestic accountability. This creates a permanent friction in a globalizing system between the logic of the economy, which is global, and the logic of politics, which is national. Accountabilities are national and in a democracy, this is reflected in the election of people to power who are running against the global capitalists. The interesting thing about American politics is that the right and the left are both now running against the global capitalist, which is very extraordinary (though neither is doing very much against them, when in power).

This makes it very difficult to maintain cooperation among governments in support of global order, global governance, and global rules for things like trade, finance, or climate. Because all the political forces acting on these institutions are national and are forcing them to pay most attention to domestic citizens. So, it takes very wise and disciplined statecraft to say to people: "We are looking after you, but cooperating globally is the best way for us to do this. We can adjust the way we cooperate globally, but we can't close off our economies, since that would impoverish us. By agreeing to do things globally, we will do better for you here at home." That is the line I would take, but it's not an easy line to sell. It's a rather sophisticated and complex argument and it looks as though you're abandoning national sovereignty. When people are frightened and angry and there are huge power shifts occurring, it's very difficult to make that sort of sophisticated argument; that the best way to achieve domestic gains is through international economic integration and cooperation.

I think Biden clearly understands this better than Trump. But even Biden knows he has to satisfy domestic constituencies that have been "losers"—not of trade, but more of domestic political changes such as the failure to get rich people and corporations to pay their fair share of taxes. It's striking that the richest people in America have the lowest tax rate. The way Biden has to deal with that is to make sure they pay taxes and to do that he has to deepen international cooperation, which is what he's trying to do on things like global corporation tax. The route to better domestic policy goes through better global policy, but this is a very sophisticated idea, which is quite difficult to sell, especially when it comes to relations with a country like China—a superpower with a very different political system.

One of the things happening on what you might broadly describe as the "somewhat populist left" in the West is that it's becoming alliance-oriented, not global. This orientation to Western alliances is fragmenting the world, not into countries, but into alliance systems. This is also dangerous by the way, but that's where it seems to be going. It's a halfway house between purely national economic sovereignty and globalization.

Meanwhile, China is working to establish itself as an advanced technology power by developing enormous strength in the technologies that the West has historically dominated, and quite a lot of Westerners regard this as threatening. So, it has become very difficult to balance national politics with global cooperation on economic and security, and that's where we are now. The most obvious period with some echoes of this one is the period of international conflict when the West dominated the world, in the late nineteenth and early twentieth centuries. That led to a complete breakdown of the world system.

Huiyao Wang: Thank you, Martin. As you summarized in your book, capitalism is global, but democracy is local. There is a tension because global capitalism has mostly benefitted elites and there has been a lack of equal opportunity. This has spawned politicians that bash globalization. To get past this, we need more international cooperation on things like addressing the pandemic or climate change. We need to work together to build trust, otherwise, we are going to be driven apart over differences in ideology and values.

In my discussions with people like Graham Allison, Joseph S. Nye Jr., and Thomas Friedman, no one has really agreed with the idea that we have entered a new "Cold War." It's a flawed analogy because China and the US are so deeply entwined. One big question is, will the rest of the world be able to recognize and accept the peaceful rise of China? Anyone who visits China can see the transformation that has occurred in the last four decades since Deng Xiaoping opened up China. China now contributes one-third of global GDP growth and is the largest trading partner of 130 countries. It is the world's leading producer of over 200 products as classified by the United Nations. Shouldn't it be possible for the rest of the world to see China's rise as a form of healthy competition, like in the Olympics, rather than insisting that only one model is the best? There may be some rivalry, but this could be "cooperative rivalry" or "rivalry partners" in the words of Joseph S. Nye Jr. and Graham Allison, respectively. Is that achievable, or are we doomed to a self-reinforcing trend toward conflict?

Martin Wolf: This is a huge question. One of the questions that I've been thinking about is, let us suppose China had a political system just like ours. Would we feel differently about it? It's a very interesting question because it's quite possible that the answer is no, though I don't think it would be a simple "no."

Such an enormous shift in the balance of global power, which you described very well, creates uncertainty and fear everywhere else. That's what the "Thucydides trap" is about and it would happen even if there were absolutely no ideological elements at all. But of course, there are, and there's also history. So, I've always assumed that some substantial degree of friction was inevitable. We just have to accept that; we do have nationally based global politics. The question is, are there any analogies from the past that help us to think about this? I agree with you completely that the Cold War is a hopeless analogy because it was an ideological competition. We had almost no economic relations between the West and the Soviet Union. They were almost completely independent entities and the Soviet Union was not really at any stage an economic rival, though it was a military rival without question. So, the Cold War is not a useful model; the West is enormously economically integrated with China and China is a huge economic power and will become a bigger one. We also share a world that we now know we have to look after together. That makes managed cooperation the only way we can possibly do this. One thing we do share with the Cold War period is that war is unthinkable. War has been unthinkable since the invention of nuclear weapons.

So, how does cooperation work? I think you must break down the elements in a pragmatic way and they have to be separated, they can't all be dealt with together. The global commons—climate, the oceans, the protection of species—are all big issues in which China will be centrally involved and will have to do a lot more than it's now planning in all these areas. That will be quite tough for China, as well as for us. That's a huge challenge but it is in China's interest too, so I think there's hope.

Then there's managing security relations in such a way that they are stable, so everybody understands what their fundamental interests are and manages them without friction. This is absolutely crucial and I don't think it's happening enough.

Then there's economics. Here I believe the West has legitimate concerns with Chinese behavior and I'm sure China has legitimate concerns with Western behavior. My own view is that both sides need to define what they regard as their core security interests in technology, which are legitimate, and they have to say that these sectors are ones where we are going to make sure we are independent. We will agree on that, and that will have impacts for trade, and we will just have to accept it. It's clear that's going to have to happen. There are core technologies both sides want to control for their own sake. Everything else should be conducted according to normal rules of trade, but those must be reciprocal and equal. I think the way Trump went about this was mad, but there is a case for a profound negotiation between China and other major powers on a new trade order, a new trade system with new rules which are more legitimate and work better. Some of these rules will be tighter and some of them will be looser, but they will be different. We can't go on as we have been and pretend the WTO system and the 2001 China accession is the last word on this economic relationship.

Then we have immensely important areas where we need to cooperate like health, development, and debt. The last is a big problem. China is a big creditor, Western countries are also big creditors. On these issues there must be active day-to-day cooperation that will require considerable changes in international organizations. This is a very broad agenda and it won't do to just go back to where we were 15 years ago. We have to move forward and that will require imaginative statecraft in the West and in China.

Huiyao Wang: Thank you. You recently wrote an article "China is wrong to think the US faces inevitable decline," which was widely read in China. You summarized the competitive strengths of the US, from universities and venture capital to corporate multinationals. One of the things I think Western countries are doing well is attracting global talent. Lee Kuan Yew, former Prime Minister of Singapore, noted how China is able to draw talent from 1.3 billion people, but that the US is able to draw on talent from 7 billion people. This is a major advantage for the US.

But China also has its competitive advantages. China's population dividend will continue for some years. China is also doing well on other things, for example, according to the global innovation index, China has 17 of the top science and technology clusters, with the Guangdong-Hong Kong-Macao Greater Bay Area and Beijing. China has also surpassed the US in terms of patents applications and Chinese universities are catching up. Each country has its relative strengths. So, while the US is doing well in terms of innovation and global multinationals, China is doing well in terms of the size of its market, which already has a middle class of 400 million people. In the next 10–15 years, China may have a middle class of 600–800 million people, which will be great for the world. It would be better if we could benefit from each other rather than attacking each other because we have different systems.

Martin Wolf: Well, we can't decouple, and we mustn't decouple. I think having deep economic relations is a good thing, both because it makes us more prosperous and also because it gives us a strong interest in one another's fate. It also leads to exchanges of ideas, knowledge, and understanding. All of these are very important.

But I also think that the reality of relations among states is always one of power. Kissinger, who after all is one of the great "bridge" individuals between the US and China, always talks about the balance of power. I think we are going to need to maintain a stable balance of power, because when it starts to be destabilized, possibilities of conflict arise—that's what Graham Allison is arguing.

One aspect of power is obviously technological. I do expect an ongoing technological rivalry. How that should work out is important, but I don't want to get into details such as whether the western attitude to Huawei made any sense—as far as I can see, it didn't. But it seems obvious that

Western powers, above all the US, are going to try and maintain technological autonomy in areas that they regard as central to their security. That's normal and can be perfectly well managed within an open world.

I also think there should be movement of people. And this may be regarded as offensive, but I think that, in terms of information flows, we're going to have to tighten up on what is allowed on our Internet, and [China] is going to have to loosen what is allowed on [the Chinese] Internet, so we are more even in that regard. The West has allowed the Internet to become a perfect medium for the dissemination of lies and this is dangerous for our stability. I also think that the level of censorship in China's system has to decline. Openness to the world, in terms of knowing what's going on, including via journalism, is very important and must be maintained on both sides. Journalists have to be allowed to report and the same applies to Chinese journalists in the West. We need to be open to one another in that fundamental respect.

I believe that in this rivalry we need to be realistic and it needs to be well managed, like a "cooperative rivalry," in such a way that everybody benefits. But the situation is not what it was 30 years ago. The other side of this is that China is now a superpower and a rising one, and will have to say to itself, "What sort of world do we want? How do we feel about the institutions of the world order? How do we interact with them? How do we want to shape them? How can we do that in ways that give other powers a sense of security and can fit in with our system?" This is a completely new challenge. The challenge for the West is obvious, as we discussed. But there's also a huge challenge for China.

Historically, for a large part of the last two to three thousand years, China was the biggest and richest place in the world. But, because of the state of technology at the time, it was largely isolated from the rest of the world, and its neighbors were much smaller. This is the first time in Chinese history that China is a great power within an integrated and interactive world. China is 1.4 billion people, but the world has about 8 billion, and there are other powers and other interests. So, China for the first time in its history is a great power, fully restored, operating within a global system that it cannot dominate. This is also true of the West and the US in particular. The West has been so used to dominating, it's now almost impossible to get used to the idea that it can't anymore. But I think the same problem, in a different way, arises with China. China must think through this: "Ok, we did incredibly well and rose to this immense stature in a world in which institutions were largely Western and in which the West thought it was dominant. That period is over. We don't accept that anymore." That's fine, but the Chinese also have to consider: How do we fit into this world? We are different, we have different political systems. Everyone is different. So, how do we make a reasonable order from *our* point of view? Do we wish to merely maintain the autonomy of the Chinese state? Do we want to create a large number of tribute states around us? How do we relate to the other great powers? What is a sensible way of doing this?

I think a lot of thinking is needed beyond the "peaceful rise." The peaceful rise has already happened. Of course, China has a long way to go—it's still relatively poor, it needs a lot of development. But China is now a leading power. I think there's a big challenge for China too in working out where China fits into the world and how it wants that world to be ordered. Take one specific example. It is pretty obvious that the World Trade Organization as it is now doesn't really work. We haven't had a successful global negotiation since 1995, except on China's accession. The WTO is not able to handle the US–China conflict. So, does China want a new system and what would it look like? I don't know. Does China think it will be OK if the system collapses? Probably not.

I think the first speech I ever gave at the China Development Forum was in 2010 and I asked, "What is China's view on the future of the trading system?" I think there is still no answer to that question. I think the same is true for the monetary system, though the previous People's Bank of China governor talked about that. I want China to be a leader. I want China to come forward with its ideas on how this new world is to run. I think that will be very challenging, it won't be the way it was in 2005. But I agree with you completely that we need to have working relations and cooperative relations, despite immense differences and frictions which will never go away, like differences over human rights. I would be very grateful for clear Chinese positions on how you want to take this forward. You hear a lot from the US, but not much from China.

I think China is at a point where we want more leadership from China. We will probably disagree, but we will disagree about real things. That's fine, I don't have any problem with that as long as it's peaceful and it's ultimately aimed at managing relations.

Huiyao Wang: I agree that China should be more active internationally. The current international order was really made by the US, like the Bretton Woods system. It is largely an English-speaking system and based on Western legal traditions, so it will take time, but I agree that China should do more.

Martin Wolf: This has been a long and very deep discussion, fair and frank too. And I've enjoyed it enormously. I believe in the management of our shared planet. It's our destiny and our duty to manage this planet in such a way that we pass it on to future generations in a good state.

There are many huge challenges and relations between China and the West will play an enormous role in determining how this plays out over the next few decades and indeed possibly centuries. I'm a Westerner and I have a very strong attachment to our core Western values, and that's inevitable, but I think I do so without any illusions about what the West has done. Western history has its faults and crimes. But I am a Westerner and I won't abandon our core values—individual liberty, law, and democracy. The great threat to that is internal, not from anyone else. Frictions of power and ideas between the West and China will continue, but I also think they're manageable because what we share is more important than what divides us. We're all human and we all want to lead better lives. We all want peace. We want our children and grandchildren to live fulfilled lives into the next century and that will demand close, intelligent corporation between China and the West. That will make big demands on both sides; we're going to have to do things differently by taking the views and interests of each other into account, in a way that is very unnatural for great powers, especially great powers that are divided in so many ways by history and culture. But I think it's possible, indeed, it is essential. The alternative is a catastrophe. If we end up in an ineradicably conflictual relationship we will not be able to manage the world and at worst, we will destroy it. So, what is at stake here is the future of everybody we care about.

Huiyao Wang: Great, thank you, Martin. You've said something very profound there; we're all human beings living on the same planet and share this "global village." We must work for a better future and manage our differences and coexist peacefully.

The World Isn't Just Flat…It's Also Fast, Fused, Deep, and Fragile

A Dialogue with Thomas L. Friedman

Huiyao Wang and Thomas L. Friedman

On March 29, 2021, CCG hosted a discussion between CCG President Huiyao Wang and *New York Times* columnist Thomas L. Friedman. Friedman is a three-time Pulitzer Prize-winning journalist and author of seven *New York Times* bestsellers—*From Beirut to Jerusalem* (1989), *The Lexus and the Olive Tree* (1999), *Longitudes and Attitudes* (2002), *The World Is Flat* (2005), *Hot, Flat, and Crowded* (2008), *That Used to Be Us* (with Michael Mandelbaum, 2011) and most recently, *Thank You for Being Late* (2016).

Friedman has become known as a leading commentator on globalization, particularly since the publication of *The World Is Flat*, which has been widely read around the world and in China. When Wang Yang, now Chairman of the National Committee of the Chinese People's Political

H. Wang (✉)
Center for China and Globalization (CCG), Beijing, China

T. L. Friedman
The New York Times, New York, NY, USA

© The Author(s) 2022
H. Wang and L. Miao (eds.), *Understanding Globalization, Global Gaps, and Power Shifts in the 21st Century*,
https://doi.org/10.1007/978-981-19-3846-7_4

51

Consultative Conference, was party secretary of Chongqing, he made the book recommended reading for officials in the city.

Originally a Middle East specialist, Friedman is a frequent visitor to China and has written many insightful articles about China's development. He previously came to speak at CCG in 2017 and also participated in a webinar as part of CCG's annual China and Globalization Forum in November 2020. I first met Thomas during my time as a visiting fellow at the Brookings Institute in 2010 and we have kept up frequent contact since then.

By March 2021 when this dialogue took place, the impact of the pandemic on various trends shaping globalization was increasingly evident. On one hand, technological innovations had allowed many workers and industries to adopt new ways of working and trade had bounced back after severe disruption in 2020. At the same time, the continued rise of populism and anti-globalization sentiment had seen some countries revert to unilateral policies and protectionism, while heated accusations over COVID-19 had exacerbated geopolitical tensions, notably between China and the US. Despite the transition to a new administration, the US remained in a period of political tumult and polarization.

Friedman was an ideal thinker to help make sense of these developments in a broader context and link them to structural shifts in society and the global economy. In our discussion, Friedman shared his latest views on topics such as the changing dimensions and drivers of globalization, how new forms of global coalitions are needed to deal with our shared challenges, underlying factors influencing China–US relations, and the ongoing impact of technological change on societies around the world. (Since this book is being published over one year later, I also asked him to add or expand on any points he made back then for this published version.) We started the dialogue by revisiting Friedman's famous claim that "the world is flat" and how globalization is changing in the post-pandemic era.

Huiyao Wang: Thomas, you've become something of an icon and symbol of globalization because of your famous book *The World Is Flat*, which is a long-time bestseller in China that has influenced many people. In that book, you talked about globalization as divided into three phases: the globalization of countries, the globalization of companies, and then the globalization of individuals. Countries have competed for thousands of years, making the world "flat" in the process. Companies have also played a great role. Since the 2000s and the Internet revolution, we see individuals playing a major role.

Today, we see globalization facing more challenges. There is more "deglobalization" and populism. So, what is your current take on globalization? How do we look at the new trends shaping globalization?

Thomas Friedman: That's a good place to start. Whenever I do webinars like this, often the first question people have is, is the world still flat? And I always start to laugh a little and say, wait a minute; I'm sitting in my office in Bethesda, Maryland, and my friend Henry is sitting in his office in Beijing, and we're having a conversation as two individuals as if we are sitting across the desk from each other. Is the world still flat? Are you crazy? It's flatter than ever. Remember, when I wrote *The World Is Flat* in 2004, Facebook didn't exist, "Twitter" was still a sound, the "cloud" was still in the sky, "4G" was a parking place, LinkedIn was a prison, Big Data was a Rap star, SKYPE was a typo and an "application" was what you sent to college, [...] All of those things came after I wrote *The World Is Flat*.

The world today is flatter than ever. We have never connected more different nodes than we have today, and we've never greased and sped up those connections more than we have today. But we've also done a third thing. We've removed a lot of the buffers that managed the flow between those nodes. Between December 2019 and March 2020, just as the Coronavirus was emerging, there were 3200 direct flights from China to America. There were 50 direct flights from Wuhan to America, and most Americans had never even heard of Wuhan.

Think about what's going on in the Suez Canal today. There's a ship stuck in the Suez Canal and there is some company in Europe waiting for its supply from China because of just-in-time inventory delivery. When we take the buffers out, the system just gets faster and faster. So, the world isn't just flat now, it's fragile. It's fragile because when you connect so many nodes and then you speed up the connection between those nodes and you take the buffers out, you get fragility. Because now I can transmit instability from my node to your node faster than ever. Since I wrote *The World Is Flat*, many people wrote books saying the world is not flat, that it's spiky, it's lumpy, it's curved, or it's bumpy. All of those books are wrong. The world is flatter than ever.

Huiyao Wang: I think that's absolutely correct, globalization is accelerating with technology. Also, the movement of capital, goods, and talent—all of these flows have become denser and faster than before.

So how do you see the future, will we see new development trends? Of course, we've seen the rise of the digital economy. And as you said, before the pandemic we had over 3000 direct flights between China and the US and there were 400,000 Chinese students in the US. Before the pandemic, China had about 150 million outbound tourists each year, with 10 million people going to Japan, another 10 million people going to Thailand, and 3 million people going to the US. So, what will we see in the future?

Thomas Friedman: The book I'm working on now, if I gave it a name and it doesn't have a name yet, is the world is not just "flat" anymore. The world is fast, fused, deep, and open. So, let's go through all four of those.

When I say the world is "fast," what I mean is that there's been a change in the pace of change. The speed of technological change now just gets faster and faster—as microchips improve and telecommunications improve—so the world is really getting "fast."

Second, the world isn't just flat now, it's "fused." We're not just interconnected, we're now *interdependent*. A ship gets stuck in the Suez Canal and something that Tom is waiting for in Bethesda and something that Henry is waiting for in Beijing are both affected. So, we're not just connected; we're fused together. We're also fused together by climate. What America does with its air affects Canada. What China does with its air can affect Thailand. What Australia does with its forest fires affects New Zealand. So, we're fused by technology and by climate.

Third, the world's gotten deep. "Deep" is the most important word of this era because we have now put sensors everywhere. For many years, for millennia, the world has been speaking to us, but we just couldn't hear it. IBM did a study a few years ago. They took a lake—Lake George—in New York state and put sensors from the surface all the way to the bottom, from one edge to the other. Suddenly, a lake that was just there—it was beautiful, we drove by it—started to "speak," started to tell us what was going on at the bottom, the middle, the next level, fish, fauna, all kinds of things. Now our knowledge of that [lake] is "deep," very deep. John Kelly, who ran IBM research at the time, told me: "Tom, the world has been speaking to us all these years—we just couldn't hear it. Now we can."

So, that's why this word "deep" is both so much more prevalent now—and so important. We had to coin a new set of adjectives—deep state, deep mind, deep medicine, deep research, deep fake, to describe the fact that this is going deep inside of me and so many other places—to depths we have never plumbed before. I can sit here right now in Washington and look at publicly available satellite pictures of different parts of China from Google Earth, from the European space satellite. I can look "deep" and I could probably find your office and see if you're coming to work. I can do that as an individual—little Tom Friedman can now go on to Google Earth and see [your] office. But I can also see into Xinjiang and China can see into Minneapolis, my hometown. So, the world is getting "deep."

Lastly, the world is getting radically open. With a smartphone, every citizen is now a paparazzi, a filmmaker, a journalist, publisher—with no editor and no filter. With a smartphone, a citizen in my hometown in Minneapolis took a video of a policeman with his knee on the neck of a man named George Floyd. One person did that with this device and George Floyd became a name that went all over the world. People in China know the name George Floyd because an individual with only a smartphone in an open world was able to tell that story. The same is true for China—we've seen that in Hong Kong and we've seen that in other areas. So, the world is getting fast, fused, deep, and open. That is the central governing challenge today. How do you govern a world that is that fast, fused, deep and, open? That is our challenge.

Huiyao Wang: Yes, this world that is faster, deeper, fused, and more open—these seem to be the new trends you're identifying for the next phase of globalization. The world is no longer just "flat," there are many other layers now. You pose a very profound question; with the world changing so fast, is [our current form of global governance] based on the Bretton Woods system built up after the Second World War equipped to cope with our new challenges?

Thomas Friedman: When the world gets this fast, fused, deep, and open, there's only one way to govern it effectively, whether that be at the national, local, or international level, and that's with what I call complex adaptive coalitions.

I take that term from nature. I think that entering a fast, fused, deep, and open world is like a big climate change. We're going through a big change in our climate; not just the "climate of the climate", but the climate of everything, of technology and globalization, etc. In nature, when an ecosystem goes through a climate change, which ecosystems thrive and survive? Those that forge complex, adaptive networks where all the parts of the system network together to maximize their resilience and their "propulsion," their ability to go forward.

This is true of the world as well. When the world gets this fast, fused, deep, and open, the only way we can govern it effectively is with global complex adaptive coalitions. We cannot manage climate change unless America, China, and Europe in particular—also India, Japan, and Korea—the big economies are all working together. Who can manage global trade now, unless all the big economies are working together? So, it's only complex adaptive coalitions that can effectively get the best out of this world and cushion us from the worst.

The problem is that right when there is a need for complex adaptive coalitions, governments are becoming more nationalistic. China's government is becoming more nationalistic. Under President Trump, America became more nationalistic. Russia, more nationalistic. Britain with Brexit, more nationalistic. Countries are becoming more nationalistic, right when we need global coalitions more than ever. Even inside countries, political parties are becoming more tribal, right when they need to be more open and collaborative. So, the world is fighting with this trend—because it challenges the old left–right binary parties in the West and the single, president-for-life strongman systems in Russia and China.

There's a whole set of issues now that can only be managed effectively with global governance: cyber, financial flows, trade, climate, and labor flows. They require global governance, but there's no global government. So, what do we do when we need global governance but there is no global government? This is the problem. And when the US and China, the two biggest countries, start fighting in the middle, the situation gets even worse.

Huiyao Wang: Exactly, I think that's a challenge we are facing. There is a lack of global governance because there's no global government. After the Second World War, we formed the UN and the Bretton Woods system, with the World Bank, IMF, and the WTO. That system has served us for 75 years. But we have seen this system is no longer sufficient, particularly given the fast pace of globalization.

It has now been 50 years since Dr. Kissinger visited China, which later led to normalized relations between China and the US. Since China joined the WTO 20 years ago, China's GDP has increased by 10–12 times. China has been able to prosper as it embraced globalization and lifted 800 million people out of poverty. But China is still often criticized in Western countries. Isn't it the case that every country has its own problems, and China also has to tackle its own problems just like the US does?

In one of your [recent columns], you wrote about how in the US, it is "Socialism for the rich" and "Capitalism for the rest." It surprised me that just 10 percent of Americans own more than 80 percent of stock wealth and have seen their wealth triple in 30 years, while the bottom wage earners have seen no gain. President Trump [liked to] blame China for this widening gap, though China actually managed to lift 800 million people out of poverty. So, do you think it is time to forge a new global consensus or some new global narratives?

Thomas Friedman: US–China relations have become very complicated, so I'll give you my view of that […] I think the four decades of US–China relations from 1979 to 2019 will go down as an epoch in US–China relations. Unfortunately, that epoch is over. So, what was that epoch about?

That epoch was a period of what I call "unconscious integration." "Unconscious" not because we weren't thinking about it, but because it was so easy. As an American company, I could say I want to have a supply chain that starts in China. As an American parent, I could say that I want my son or daughter to go to university in China to study Mandarin. As an employer, I could say I want to hire the best Chinese technologist or student living in America. On the Chinese side, any Chinese could say over time, I want my company listed on the Nasdaq, I want to have an American partner, or I want my kid to go to school in America.

Over those 40 years, China and America became in some ways, the real "one country, two systems." We really got fused together. Now, that era, unfortunately, is over. Why is it over? Well, I come back to the word "deep" because for most of those 30–40 years, China sold us mostly "shallow" goods—clothes we wore on our shoulders, shoes we wore on our feet, solar panels we put on our roof. I call those "shallow" goods. At the same time, we sold China "deep goods"—things like computers, software, things that went right inside your office. So, for the most part, the US sold China "deep" things and China sold the US "shallow" things. And China had to buy our deep goods because for many years it could not make its own.

When China sold the US only "shallow" things, politically speaking, we didn't care whether China was authoritarian, communist, libertarian, or vegetarian. It didn't matter, because you were just selling us shallow goods. But China, by its own technological development, over the last

10 years is now able to make deep goods such as Huawei with 5G. Now, Chinese firms come to America and want to sell deep goods, just like the US sold China deep goods. They want to sell Tom Friedman Huawei products that will go in his house, answer his telephone.

When China was just selling the US shallow goods, we didn't care about your political system. But if China wants to sell deep goods to me here in Bethesda, if you want Huawei to answer my phone, suddenly the difference in values matters. That's where the absence of shared trust between our two countries now really matters. China's central value is the stability of the collective. So, if the collective is advancing, if more people are coming out of poverty, that is a central Chinese value; that is valued more than the right to religious and cultural expression for the Uyghurs in Xinjiang and it is valued more than a relatively small number of people getting super-rich. China's focus has always been on the collective and stability because China has 1.4 billion people. I wish there was more tolerance in China for individual and group cultural and ideological differences—and the right to express them. I believe that China would be enriched by embracing that diversity.

In America, we put much more primacy on the individual: the right of the individual to express themselves, the right of the individual to start a company, the right of the individual to thrive and do better—or worse. So, when a nation values the right of the individual, that means the primacy of human rights and individual rights.

So, suddenly, in a deep world, Americans can look into Google Earth and see what look like forced labor camps in Xinjiang, and say—wait a minute, I can see deep inside of China now—and how you are treating your Muslim population, that bothers me. And China can say—wait a minute, I'm looking at what's going on in Minnesota or Minneapolis, and how you have large numbers of poor people—maybe that bothers me too? Now, we can look inside Hong Kong. From my office, I can see if China is not living up to its obligations to allow more democracy in Hong Kong.

Now, we're having a clash on values in a way we didn't during that 40-year epoch. That's going to be a problem because our difference in values is now making things very complicated. Because China is now wealthier and more powerful, it's also able to assert itself and its values more powerfully at home and abroad. So, we have a lot of work to do. The big question is, can we get back to a joint project, a shared project? Because for the relative peace and prosperity of the world for those 40 years from

1979 to 2019, at the core was China–US relations, that US–China "one country, two systems." If we rip that apart, the world will not be as prosperous and it will not be as peaceful. And as the world gets fast, fused, deep, and open, it won't be governed the way it needs to be.

So, we need to have some very deep conversations. China needs to understand that in a deep world, I can see inside Xinjiang. If I think that there's forced labor there, I may boycott your cotton. Americans need to understand that a country of 1.4 billion people needs to maintain stability, that's a high priority, and that it's going to come at this in a different way. We have to have an honest conversation on this.

Huiyao Wang: Absolutely, I agree that we need deep dialogue. That's the purpose of this conversation as well. You are right, we have to look at values. But we also should also forge some new narratives. In the last 40 years, China has opened up and changed beyond recognition. Any foreigner that came to China 30 or 40 years ago would recognize these great changes. This year, the Chinese government has announced that they have lifted 800 million people out of poverty, completed the 13th Five-Year Plan, and the CPC's first centennial goal of becoming a "moderately prosperous society." China is now launching the 14th Five-Year Plan and by 2035 China will double its GDP, working one five-year plan after another.

I remember when the former US Ambassador to China, Terry Branstad, invited me to his farewell cocktail event, he said that he thought that the success of China can be attributed to three factors. One is that the Chinese are really hard-working, because any time you come to China, it's not "9 to 5" but probably more like "9/9/6" [the practice of working from 9 a.m. until 9 p.m., 6 days a week]. The second factor is that Chinese people attach great importance to family values and have great respect for seniors and collectivism. The third factor is education; in China, a family often has only one child, and the whole family values education.

China's success is not really built on a traditional orthodox system as some Americans may understand it. It is a system that now combines technology, consultative democracy, the market economy, and meritocracy. China has delivered when it comes to actual performance. As Deng Xiaoping said, it doesn't matter if the cat is black or white, as long as it catches mice. So, if China can lift 800 million people out of poverty and minimize casualties from COVID-19, those are also major human rights achievements, given the situation. As you said, China has 1.4 billion people, so stability has always been important. China has also built two-thirds of the world's high-speed rail network, has seven out of the top 10 largest ports in the world, has become the largest trading partner of 130 countries, and contributes over one-third to global GDP growth.

In terms of "KPIs," China is doing well. So, maybe we should be a little more tolerant of different systems. As President Biden said, we can have competition between the US and China, even fierce competition, but we should also cooperate. As Chinese Foreign Minister Wang Yi said at the National People's Congress, we should have peaceful competition and cooperation. Shouldn't we treat each other as equals and avoid getting into a Cold War-type situation? I think this is the way that a lot of people in China think.

Thomas Friedman: It's a very good point. People said to me, if you're going on a webinar in China, they must be censoring. I said, no—I'll bring up human rights violations Xinjiang, I'll bring up democracy in Hong Kong. Nobody's going to censor me.

We're having a valuable dialogue—you're giving me China's perspective and I'm giving you the concerns of America. Having a respectful dialogue is so important. What worries me most is that there are only around three American journalists left in China. China has basically thrown out almost all the Western journalists. America has asked some Chinese journalists to leave too, though not as many as China. So, we're not having this respectful dialogue.

You've got your perspective, which is not illegitimate from my point of view. The points you raise about bringing people out of poverty and providing stability—these things also really do affect the human condition. You listen respectfully to my perspective when I raise questions about how a whole culture is treated in Xinjiang or democracy in Hong Kong. Then maybe you'll come back and say, Tom's got a point, and I come back and say, Henry's got a point.

In a respectful dialogue, I can say to you: if China did this particular thing on Hong Kong, or in Xinjiang, it would really help. And you could say: Tom, if America did this particular thing regarding how the US talks about China, how the US treats China in the world, it would really help. Maybe then we could start to take confidence-building measures where each of us does something to lower the temperature. Unfortunately, what happened in Alaska in the US–China talks in March 2021 was more like mutual name-calling which just left everybody feeling kind of raw and angry.

So, I want to say that I appreciate the respectful dialogue that you're hosting. I wish we could broaden this because there are legitimate concerns that America and the West have, and I'm afraid that those legitimate concerns aren't even listened to. What I fear, though I don't hope for this, is that we'll end up in something like a boycott of the 2022 Olympics, and then the whole relationship will blow up.

That's why I think it's so important that we have a dialogue [in which] China says, I hear you, I will take this gesture, and America says I hear you, I will take this gesture. And we find ways to work together. Because in a fused world, as my friend Graham Allison always says, we now have mutually assured destruction. The US and China can destroy each other, we can destroy the global economy, we can destroy the global climate. So, we are doomed to work together. What bothers me right now is that we're not having the kind of frank but respectful dialogue that we need and then walking away from that dialogue with a to-do list, so that [Henry thinks] "I've heard what Tom says about the situation of the Uighurs or Hong Kong, I don't agree with all of it, but I'm going to try to work on something." And I come away and say, "I hear what Henry is saying, that this country brought 800 million people out of poverty. Do you know how much more stable the world is because China did that? That's also a huge thing. So, I'm going to work on things that are of your concern."

We need to get back to that dialogue because going back to my central point, the 40 years from 1979 to 2019 will be seen as a golden era of relative global prosperity and peace, and the core of it was the US and China. If you rip out that core, China's diplomats may have a good day putting America down, and US diplomats may have one good day putting China down. But the world will have a bad year, year after year, if we don't find a way for the US and China to work together.

Huiyao Wang: Yes, I think as the largest two economies in the world, China and the US have a moral responsibility to work together. I agree that journalism should be resumed. The consulates that have been shut down should be reopened and we should expand [people-to-people] exchanges. China has about 400,000 students in the US, but the US has only about 10,000 in China, so I hope that we can attract more US students to China. On the social and civil society level, we could have more exchange.

You raised issues such as Xinjiang and Hong Kong. The feeling here is that we often hear international voices say, [China] has 1, 2, or even

3 million Uighurs locked up, but we don't know where that number is coming from. Where is the source of these statistics? Or [outside observers] say they have identified so many buildings via satellite. But many of these buildings are empty, they aren't really housing many people. Another thing is that there are only 10–12 million Uighurs in Xinjiang, so it is [difficult to claim] there are really 1–3 million Uighurs locked up. The Chinese government stated in its white paper last year that all of the trainees in education school have graduated already. The Xinjiang government has said that again this year. The Chinese Foreign Ministry's spokesperson has welcomed foreign ambassadors and journalists to [visit Xinjiang]. I think the best way, as you said, is to have more dialogue and exchange, rather than talking about each other and not talking to each other.

The same is true with Hong Kong. Hong Kong is no longer in a chaotic situation—the stock market has [bounced] back, multinationals have come back. The Legislature Council is safe now. We really need a lot of dialogue on these issues and need to welcome all journalists on both sides to promote this dialogue.

Thomas Friedman: I think it'd be very important, from my point of view, if a team of *New York Times* reporters was allowed into Xinjiang. Let them go, let them write, let them see. Then we can draw an independent conclusion. I think that's very important. And from the Chinese side too—anywhere you want to come in America, I think you should be allowed to go.

Huiyao Wang: I think that could be a good idea. It can be open and I think openness is a great way to solve all these questions. At the China Development Forum [in March 2021] you also mentioned decoupling. I think it is very hard to decouple. You talked about Huawei and how maybe we should let Huawei experiment in some more remote US states, so as to build up trust like you said. Trust building between us should be given a new start during the new Biden administration.

Thomas Friedman: I feel very strongly about that because if we go to a tech cold war, I believe that will be bad not only for the world but also bad for America. If there is a Chinese tech ecosystem and an American tech ecosystem, I'm not sure the majority of the world will come to the American tech ecosystem, either for financial reasons or technological reasons.

I don't think decoupling is a healthy thing, I think the best thing in the world is mutual interdependence. I want China dependent on Intel chips and I'm totally comfortable if America is dependent on Chinese supply chains. I think the more interdependent we become, the more the politics will follow. As I've said before, I've been going to China now since 1989. China is so much more open than it was 30–40 years ago and I would say it's more closed than it was 5–6 years ago. But I also believe the trend line is for China to develop and build a bigger and bigger middle class. People don't just come out of poverty but enter the middle class. How many Chinese tourists now are coming out into the world? Tens of millions every year. So, people say to me sometimes, "Friedman, you said China would become more open, but in the last five or six years, it's become more closed." I said, well, who declared the year 2021 the end of history? Countries move at different paces, like three steps forward and half a step back. I am confident that as China develops—not just out of poverty, but also grows a middle class that wants to travel—and as Chinese students go all over the world, the trend line toward openness will continue. We should have a little confidence in that, too. I think the more we integrate, the more that will happen. But we do have this core trust problem.

One of the things I often ask myself is "what are we fighting about?" It's surely not ideology, because in many ways China is more capitalist than we are. Does China want to take over Chinatown in San Francisco? I don't think so. Does America want to occupy Shanghai or Nanjing? I don't think so. I'm not even sure what we're fighting about. In the deepest sense, yes there's a clash of values, I get that. Obviously, it's two great powers who have influence, but this all should be manageable.

It does require each of us to do something hard. Like China undertaking confidence-building measures on Xinjiang or on Hong Kong. Or the West taking hard confidence-building measures on something like Huawei, where America can give a test like allowing China to install 5G in Texas, and we'll see how you do. And if you do better, then you can go to Oklahoma, if you behave in accordance with our laws.

To get each other's attention, China and the US each have to do something hard. When China does something hard in Hong Kong and Xinjiang, that will really get Americans' attention. And when we do something hard on something like Huawei, that will get China's attention. That's something we can then build on. Right now, neither side wants to really do anything hard, because for us, to let Huawei in now would politically be hard. For China to take the kind of steps to respect human rights that we've been talking about in Xinjiang or Hong Kong will be hard. But if we each do something hard now, that would have a huge impact to build confidence. That would be the thing that would really change the direction of the relationship right now.

Huiyao Wang: I think the trust and confidence-building that you talked about are absolutely important. You really hit the point with that question, "what are we fighting for?" What is the point of fighting when our two countries are so intertwined? The US–China Business Council issued a report not too long ago which estimated that the trade war could cause a drop of 0.5 percent in America's GDP and the loss of 2–300,000 jobs in the US. Many Western automobile companies sell more cars in China than in their own countries and Tesla has maintained full production and had a very profitable year in China despite the COVID-19 pandemic. Walmart purchases many goods from China and China is the second-largest market for Apple after the US, so the two countries are very much intertwined.

Thomas Friedman: Absolutely. China is the second-largest book market for me, I sold more copies of *The World Is Flat* in China than in any other country other than America. So, I know the benefits of our integration. There will be trade issues and questions of fairness that are very serious and which we need to address, but we need to get away from the kind of meeting, which took place in Alaska, get away from public name-calling, and get down to some hard "doing" rather than just "hard talk." That's what will actually change the dynamic in the relationship.

Huiyao Wang: That's right. I saw that at the recent Munich Security Conference [in February 2021]. President Biden didn't talk about US–China "rivalry" but rather "competition." He said the US doesn't seek confrontation with China. And China always emphasizes peaceful coexistence.

Thomas Friedman: I must point out the fact that President Xi and President Biden have a personal relationship, which is very unusual. I was actually at the State Department lunch and got to sit at the table when both of them were vice presidents and got to see that personal relationship. We must not waste that. But it has been under a lot of stress lately.

Huiyao Wang: Absolutely [...] Recently, the Ford Foundation and quite a few US foundations have restarted their US–China scholar exchange programs. We hope that the Fulbright Scholarship Program, the US Consulate in Chengdu, and other student exchange programs can resume operations too. I notice there are some changes in tone with the

Biden administration. They are not attacking the CPC on a daily basis anymore and they are more pragmatic. They are not arresting people and charging them with espionage or labeling Chinese students as spies. As you said, there is a lot both sides can do. If we all value certain things, such as the peace and prosperity of the world, then we should be able to abandon certain outdated mindsets, look at the facts, and focus on how to run our own countries effectively.

At present, it seems like there are two main points of bipartisan consensus in the US Congress. One is on China and the other is on infrastructure. The US needs to renovate its infrastructure and China is a world leader in infrastructure development. It has the longest high-speed rail network, the longest highway system, and 80 percent of the world's tallest bridges. So, maybe the US and China can collaborate on infrastructure. You mentioned Texas; the cost of exporting energy from inland Texas to China is double compared to importing from the coastal areas of Texas because of inadequate infrastructure in the state. China and the US could work together to fill infrastructure gaps such as this. In addition, the Asian Infrastructure Investment Bank (AIIB) could be elevated into a "World" Infrastructure Investment Bank, in which the US and Japan could participate.

Your recent column in *The New York Times*, "China doesn't respect us anymore—for good reason," drew a lot of attention. But I want to ask, if the shoe doesn't fit China, how could China have made such great achievements? Of course, globalization is a factor, but with its 5,000-year history, China has its own culture and logic of development. For example, amidst a situation like the pandemic, it's a society where people are willing to sacrifice a certain amount of individual freedom for collective benefits. But these are more cultural differences rather than ideological differences and we probably need to be more careful when we consider the nature of our differences and not overstate them.

Thomas Friedman: For me, 90 percent of US' China policy is about making America stronger. That is, if we invest in our infrastructure, if we invest in our education, if we invest in government-funded research, if we take advantage of immigration, which is one of the great advantages we've always had over every other country, namely that we can attract the world's best brains to our shores, including Chinese, we will be much more self-confident in how we deal with China; we will be able to negotiate from a position of strength.

So, we need to get our own act together. I believe we have some legitimate differences—moral, diplomatic, and ethical differences—that have informed our critiques of China over how it has dealt with Hong Kong's democracy, Xinjiang's Muslims, and cyberattacks on US institutions. I make no apologies for those. We must always raise those issues from our side. But we have got to get our act together at home. That's what I was saying in that article. China has a formula for success. We had a formula for success, but we've gotten away from our formula for success. If we are the most dynamic, attractive, and compelling economy and society in the world, to me, that's the best China policy and the best Russia policy, because their people will look at us and say, "we want more of that." One good example is worth a thousand theories.

I get criticized a lot because when I point out how well China is doing on education, infrastructure, or science, people say, "Friedman, you love China."

But actually, I'm not really thinking about China, I'm thinking about America. Very frankly, I'm trying to use China's success on infrastructure, on education, on science, and on anti-poverty as a way to stimulate and challenge Americans. During the Cold War, why did we build a highway system? Because we thought we needed it to win the Cold War against the Russians. Why did we race to the moon? Because we thought we needed to race with the Russians. When we lost that foreign challenger, frankly, we got a little lazy at home and we were ready to settle—as I said in that article, to be "dumb as we wanna be." So, I'm not at all ashamed of taking China's successes and saying to Americans—they're going to be the leading and most powerful country in the world if we don't get back to our formula for success. So that is my very unapologetic strategy of pointing out that China is succeeding. I don't want China to fail. I think the world will be better if China succeeds and the US succeeds at the same time. Being the best example is the most powerful human rights policy, the most powerful democracy-promotion policy, the most powerful economic policy, and the most powerful diplomatic policy. Believe me, the world will respond.

Huiyao Wang: That is very stimulating. You mentioned that one of the core advantages of the US is the ability to attract talent. Perhaps the Biden administration will do more on that front, such as welcoming foreign students. Graham Allison told me how the former prime minister of Singapore Lee Kuan Yew said to him, the US is picking talent from 7 billion people and China is picking talent from 1.3 billion people. So,

[China] really has to learn from the US as well and perhaps attract more US students to come to China. We need to do more to increase mutual understanding and trust. At the moment, there are not many people in the US that really understand China well. You are an exception as you know so much about China, and we hope that we can hold more dialogues like this.

The US and China, as the two largest countries in the world, have to work together. We should work to ensure that the bilateral relationship is one of peaceful competition rather than confrontation and rivalry. China and the US have their differences, but it is important that we build up a more transparent rules-based system to manage the competition. For example, China and the US should work together to reform the World Trade Organization (WTO). CCG is also promoting the idea that China should join the Comprehensive and Progressive Agreement for Trans-Pacific Partnership (CPTPP) and Chinese leaders have said that China is willing to join CPTPP, which is a high-standard trade pact designed by the US. So, rather than fighting through trade and tariffs, we could instead discuss and negotiate through multilateral mechanisms such as the WTO and CPTPP or through the bilateral investment treaty that the US and China almost concluded during the Obama administration.

Thomas Friedman: I have visited CCG many times and have always appreciated the forum that you have given me, where I can be very frank. Whenever I've spoken, I've spoken my mind. I have benefited from you speaking your mind very honestly in defending your system and I do the same.

This is my message. You only get one chance to make a second impression. Not the first impression; you only have one chance to make a second impression. China and America really need to make a second impression on each other right now. We both need to give each other a second look. I think that will only happen if we each do something a little hard, so that people say, "Wow, that was hard for China to do" and "that was hard for America to do." We need to get each other's attention again.

I want to give this friendly advice to Chinese diplomats. You don't want to be seen as a bully. When a country like Australia just asks China to investigate where Covid-19 came and Beijing's response is to impose economic sanctions on Australia for just asking, that's bullying. Nobody likes a bully, and you know how I know that? Because nobody liked America to be a bully. After the Cold War, we thought we were the "hyperpower" and could go anywhere and tell anyone to do anything.

Some people in Latin America and Southeast Asia thought we were kind of a big bully and nobody likes a bully. What people like and what people really respond to is when they see you do something hard. We need to do that and China needs to do that, and then we can both have a second impression.

Huiyao Wang: There is a better way to tell the story of China, absolutely. I was glad to see that US Secretary of State Blinken said that the US no longer needs to topple other governments. This paves the way for more peaceful coexistence. China and the US need each other to maintain global stability.

Thomas Friedman: I think what happened in Alaska was a necessary throat-clearing for both sides. Both sides needed to clear their throats. Joe Biden is a good man, he's a stable president, he is not like Trump. He's a partner for serious dialogue and I'm still hopeful that now both sides have got everything off their chest, they can sit down and have the kind of dialogue that you and I are having, which is honest, frank, and respectful, but also a dialogue where we actually agree to do something and bring the relationship where it needs to be.

Huiyao Wang: You are right. We needed to clear our throats and then we can really calm down and talk about important matters.

To finish off, I have a question for you referring back to globalization. Due to the pandemic, people in different countries are isolated from each other. Many companies and organizations are stagnating. Do you think these factors will slow down globalization or do you think globalization will have a new start after COVID-19?

Thomas Friedman: A very good question and a good place to end. I think we are on the verge of an incredible explosion of globalization because of what the pandemic has done. Before the pandemic, McKinsey estimated that about 20 percent of American companies had digitized their business. After the pandemic, so many more companies have digitized their business. Look what CCG has done—you've digitized your forums. Now, you and I are acting globally as individuals more easily, more cheaply, and more efficiently than ever. It's not as good as when I'm in your auditorium but it's about 90 percent as good. When I'm in your auditorium, we just have the people in the auditorium, but now we have 800,000 people around China watching.

So, you see that the pandemic has forced us to digitize many things and is also going to allow us to globalize in so many more ways, such as tele-medicine, tele-education, and tele-business. What will come out of this is a new hybrid. So next time you and we meet, maybe it'll be on Zoom, or maybe it'll be in your office in Beijing, or maybe it'll be in your office in Beijing with Zoom. I think when this is over, we will have so many more ways to globalize. But the world is going to continue going from size "large" to "medium" to "small." Thanks to the pandemic, this is going to happen faster than ever.

Huiyao Wang: Yes, the pandemic has probably brought people closer through technology.

Thomas Friedman: I have done more webinars and have reached more people in China during the year of the pandemic than in the previous 30 years combined.

Huiyao Wang: Glad to see the positive side of it. I was also glad to see that during the Alaska meeting, both US and Chinese government officials talked about the prospect of relaxing visas and opening borders. So, we hope we can invite you again to talk with us at CCG. This kind of constructive dialogue can help to forge a better narrative as we seek common ground and try to minimize our differences. China and US, as the world's two largest economies, have a great responsibility to work together to fight climate change and the pandemic, resolve debt issues, and so many other things.

Thomas Friedman: That's absolutely correct and I have great respect for the fact that you invite me, you let me say (and I say) whatever I want, even if that includes some hard things for Chinese officials to hear, but I think it's said out of respect and a desire to see the relationship get on a healthier track. I appreciate you giving me this opportunity to reach your audience and reach so many friends and readers in China. I look forward to doing it again as I really respect and appreciate this opportunity.

Huiyao Wang: Thank you very much, Tom, for spending your time with us and we hope to see you again.

Bridging Gaps and Deficits

Understanding Inequality in a Globalizing World

A Dialogue with Angus Deaton, Anne Case, and David Blair

Huiyao Wang, Angus Deaton, Anne Case, and David Blair

On May 13, 2021, CCG hosted a dialogue between Huiyao Wang, CCG President; David Blair, CCG Vice President and Senior Economist; Anne Case, Alexander Stewart 1886 Professor of Economics and Public Affairs, Emeritus at Princeton University; and Angus Deaton, Senior Scholar, Princeton School of Public and International Affairs.

Anne Case is a world-renowned economist who has written extensively about health outcomes over the life cycle. She was previously awarded the Kenneth J. Arrow Prize in Health Economics from the International Health Economics Association for her work on the links between economic status and health in childhood. She was also awarded the Cozzarelli Prize by the National Academy of Sciences for her research on midlife morbidity and mortality.

H. Wang (✉) · D. Blair
Center for China and Globalization (CCG), Beijing, China

A. Deaton · A. Case
Princeton University, Princeton, NJ, USA

H. Wang and L. Miao (eds.), *Understanding Globalization,
Global Gaps, and Power Shifts in the 21st Century*,
https://doi.org/10.1007/978-981-19-3846-7_5

Sir Angus Deaton is a leading authority on poverty, inequality, health, well-being, and economic development. In 2015, he was awarded the Nobel Memorial Prize in Economic Sciences for his analysis of consumption, poverty, and welfare. He previously served as President of the American Economic Association. His current research focuses on the determinants of health in rich and poor countries, as well as on the measurement of poverty and inequality in the US, India, and around the world.

For this discussion, we were also joined by CCG Vice President David Blair, an economist specializing in finance, macroeconomics, entrepreneurship, and healthcare. Before joining CCG, David was a professor of economics at the Eisenhower School of the National Defense University in Washington and a senior business columnist for China Daily.

Issues of inequality within and between countries are a subject of intense debate and also feed into policy discussions related to globalization. Case and Deaton are co-authors of the book *Deaths of Despair and the Future of Capitalism* (2020), which sheds light on factors that have made life more difficult for less educated working people in America and contributed to a fall of life expectancy. Our discussion covered major themes from this book, including the role of healthcare, education, globalization, market regulation, and social changes in rising inequality in the US. We also explored the lessons that can be drawn for other countries facing serious inequality, including China.

Huiyao Wang: The book I have in my hands is *Deaths of Despair and the Future of Capitalism*, co-authored by Professor Deaton and Professor Case and published last year. Before we get into that, maybe you can both say a few words and introduce the book to our audience.

Angus Deaton: When we first started this work in the summer of 2013, we noticed this reversal in midlife mortality, of people in their 40s and 50s. For more than a century, mortality had generally been in decline. But instead of continuing to go down from the mid-1990s until when we were writing, it had started to rise. This is something you really don't expect to see at all. We didn't know at the time that overall life expectancy was falling.

Anne Case: But this was only happening in the US. In other wealthy countries, other English-speaking countries, mortality rates continued to fall. Progress was continuing elsewhere. But in the US, in one particular group of whites, the most privileged group in the US in general, mortality rates had started to rise and this came as a surprise to us and all of the other people that we showed it to. It was a shock, so that was the beginning. We started to dig to try to find out what was going on here and why did progress stop—not just for a year, but for over two decades.

Angus Deaton: Right, it was such a shock at the time. We had a lot of trouble getting the paper published. Eventually, we did get it published and there was just a tsunami of interest in it. I like to tell the story that I got the Nobel Prize in October of 2015, and there's a huge amount of publicity that comes with that, but this paper then came out two weeks later and the publicity around this paper was just huge, compared even with what had happened with the Nobel Prize. So, we knew we had really put our finger on a nerve and that people were very excited and distressed about it.

Huiyao Wang: *Deaths of Despair and the Future of Capitalism* is a fascinating book. So basically, life expectancy in the US fell for the first time in decades. It fell in 2015, 2016, and 2017. The US is one of the wealthiest countries in the world and has achieved a high life expectancy, so this trend brings lessons for other countries to learn. What can we learn from the US?

Angus Deaton: This might not be very helpful, but one of the things to say is that some of the things that happened in the US do not happen elsewhere. We draw an analogy in the book with what happened in China in the nineteenth century, when opium dealers from Britain forced their way into selling opium to the Chinese people, very much against local wishes. To some extent, there's a parallel with what happened in the US; very powerful pharmaceutical companies and pharmaceutical distributors distributed enormous amounts of opioids, essentially legalized heroin, which caused terrific trouble in the US, with many people dying.

Anne Case: The three causes of death that were rising that caused mortality to turn the wrong way in the US were suicide, drug overdose, and alcoholic liver disease. As a shorthand, we call those "deaths of despair." In those three causes of death, what we saw was a great deal of despair, because people don't kill themselves with drugs, alcohol, or a gun unless something is going very badly wrong in their lives.

So, in the book what we did was first to document that this was indeed happening throughout the US—but only for people who were not well educated, people who did not have a four-year college degree. From there, we turned to economics to ask the question—what is it that's happened in the US, that has happened only to people without a four-year college degree, that might be a powerful enough force such that people would start killing themselves in very large numbers?

Angus Deaton: A very important part of that story was that it *wasn't* happening in other rich countries around the world. Or, if it was happening, and it is happening a little in Britain, Canada, and Ireland, it's not happening on anything like the same scale as in the US. Which means that stories about globalization or technical change, which many people tend to blame, can't really explain why globalization and technical change are having such different effects in Germany and Britain than in the US.

David Blair: Could I ask you to delve a little bit deeper into the deep causes? I was very struck by your statement a minute ago that you want other countries to be able to draw on the lessons of what the US suffered and not to repeat the same mistakes. I never thought I'd be looking back on the 1970s as a kind of a golden age, but at that time, real median real wages were going up, and they haven't risen since 1979. Do you think policy changes, environmental changes, or social changes were driving it? Was it a change in society, a failure to enforce anti-monopoly laws, or changes in the financial system? There are various hypotheses and I'd just like you to elaborate on what you think the major causes were.

Angus Deaton: Well, almost all of the above. A lot of bad things were happening, the question really is to establish what caused what. There's been a lot of social disintegration, which Robert D. Putnam famously wrote about in *Bowling Alone*. He wrote to us and said that he thought the title of our book was the best title he'd seen in many years. Anne can talk about some of the other things that are happening—the morbidity, the pain, lack of marriage, churchgoing, and so on, but we tend to push it back to the labor market.

Anne Case: The high watermark for blue-collar wages in the US was in 1972. Since then, median wages for people without a college degree have been falling—for men first, for women with a lag, but they've been falling now for a couple of decades as well.

Angus Deaton: Wages rise in booms, so it's not a continuous fall. You get this ratchet effect that wages rise a bit in the boom and then they fall and never get back to where they were before. In the Trump boom, which many people pushed as being the best labor market seen in this century, real wages for people without a four-year college degree were lower than at any date in the 1980s.

Anne Case: Part of that was certainly globalization and automation, which made blue-collar workers more vulnerable. Part of it is a policy decision about whether or not the workers who were affected were going to be retrained, whether or not the pie that was getting bigger through globalization was going to be distributed to everyone, or if it was going to be just distributed among the people at the top.

So, part of that is policy. But the other part that's different about the US is the way that we finance our healthcare system. That plays an important role in the story, which is kind of happening behind the curtain because we tie health insurance to employers in the US, which is highly unusual. If you combine that with the fact that the healthcare industry got larger and larger and more and more expensive, what that meant was that employers had to pay a larger and larger premium to hire any worker, including blue-collar workers, and that came out of blue-collar wages. So, healthcare went from being not much of GDP back in, say, 1960, to being one dollar in five by the time we get to 2020. That meant blue-collar wages fell as more money was spent on their healthcare.

Angus Deaton: And the jobs went with those wages. If you're an employer, and you offer health insurance, you have to pay an additional $20,000 a year for a family policy or $11,000 a year for a single policy to hire a janitor or a cleaner. This means very few large firms in America have any cleaning staff; the mailroom is gone, the security staff, the food service workers, the drivers—they're nearly all are contracted out to local firms that supply labor.

David Blair: I was struck by a number, the share of GDP going to capital and labor. Back when I was in graduate school 30 or 40 years ago, that was considered fixed. But it's been declining. The share of GDP going to labor has declined to 7 or 8 percent over the last 30 or 40 years in the US, which is a big change. Can you talk about what's going on there?

Angus Deaton: This is a very hot area in labor economics and for those who study firms, and there's no agreement as to exactly what those forces are. And it's not clear that the same thing is happening elsewhere. I'm working with a group in London and we've spent a lot of time looking at the British labor share of GDP and some people think it's fallen, but others think it has not fallen as much.

One of the themes in this work, and I don't really want to tell you the answer because I don't think we know, is that market power plays a much bigger role than economists used to think it did. So, there's a lot of wondering about whether there's more monopsony than we used to think, with firms having power over their workers, or a lot more monopoly, with firms having power over product prices. Another factor is the decline in unions, which has happened pretty much everywhere, but has happened very fast in the US, so there are almost no private-sector unions left.

David Blair: I'm struck by how much more competitive many market sectors are in China than in the US. I just bought a car and it's an extremely highly competitive market sector for cars here, and the price is maybe two-thirds of the price of an equivalent car in the US.

Anne Case: Car dealers are very well protected by local and central governments in the US. There are regulations that help protect those sellers. It's not just cars, there are so many areas where corporations and heads of industry groups have gone to Washington or their state capitals and gotten protection. So, if you're working within a politically protected sector, you do very well, but that means that the people who aren't protected are paying the price for that.

Huiyao Wang: The question I want to pose is on the future of capitalism, which is also covered in the book. You have raised many interesting points on education, such as how people with a four-year college education tend to earn more. In China's latest census, data shows that 218 million people have a college degree or are currently in college. This will help their futures too, if we draw on the lessons of your book.

Second, on health. It is striking that the US spends almost 20 percent of its GDP on healthcare. China spends about 5 percent of GDP on healthcare and has almost 1.3 billion people with some kind of medical coverage. Life expectancy in China is only two or three years less than it is in the US and quickly catching up. Also, the role of the family. Regarding Chinese family values, there tends to be encouragement and support from the family, which may help to prevent some desperate outcomes. What do you think about how China has done and are there lessons we can draw from the US experience?

Anne Case: There are several things to pick up on here. Just to start with education, other countries don't seem to have this strict divide in social and economic treatment between whether you have a college degree or you don't, and if you have a college degree, you are protected from a deteriorating labor market, whereas if you don't have a college degree, your opportunities are declining, and it's getting harder to get married, and it's hard to have a community life that's meaningful. In other countries, that's not happening to anything like the same extent. So, it seems like that is in some way special to the US. It may be that in other countries, there's not the same stigma attached to having a meaningful job that you need skills for but you don't need a college degree for. So that's one thing.

Angus Deaton: This education thing is very hard and there's a lot of controversy about it. What you were saying about the progress that China has made in educating people, that's got to be good—we believe in education. You know, we are college professors, how could we not believe in education? Both of us grew up in pretty humble backgrounds, and for us, the educational system was our escape. It was what allowed us to do the things we've done in our lives. So, we're not going to say anything bad about education. Education gives people skills or allows latent skills to be expressed and that's good for them, and it's good for the country, and it's good for everybody, so that's a terrific thing.

But there's another role of education, which seems to be as a marker of social status. Having a BA in America seems to increasingly have become what the philosopher Michael Sandel has called the key to respect, the key to social esteem, and the key to a good job. That has a big downside as well as an upside. So, we're not going to badmouth education, but it's more the role that this BA degree has come to play in the US which I think has been problematic.

Anne Case: To pick up on family values, in America, conservatives like to point to the erosion of family values; that people are no longer industrious and that people no longer have a moral compass that says, "we live in a family and we take care of our family." Instead, they point out that we have people cohabiting, they break up, they may have had a child in their first cohabitation, and then they have a new cohabitation, they have another child, and their home life is often very fragile. But in the book, we point out that it's much easier to be virtuous if you have a good job—if you have a job where you have prospects, where there's on the job training, where you feel like you have a future—it's much easier to support a lifestyle that's stable if you feel that you have status, meaning you know that work is going to lead you to a good life.

Angus Deaton: There's an old Marxist belief that social relations depend on the means of production and that seems to be what's happening here. We see the disintegration of these patterns where people used to have good working-class blue-collar jobs as being behind this social disintegration.

Huiyao Wang: I'd like to raise another question about inequality. We notice inequality around the world as globalization deepens. For example, the wealth of the top 1 percent in the US is almost equal to 42 percent to 45 percent of the wealth of the whole population. Many developed countries show the same trend. As companies expand globally, it seems they're not sufficiently benefiting their home or host countries. For example, the North American Free Trade Agreement [NAFTA] was blamed for hollowing out the Midwest and not benefiting the US. Martin Wolf points out how capitalism is global, whereas democracy is local. So, if the local population is not happy, politicians seek out a scapegoat, which is often China.

What do you think about this inequality issue, particularly during the pandemic, when we see the top 1 percent getting even wealthier and the stock market at an all-time high? How can we explain this and what are the challenges for our contemporary world?

Angus Deaton: I think you have to be careful to separate different kinds of inequality. There's inequality in income, which is what perhaps we first think about, and then there is wealth inequality, which some politicians in the US such as Elizabeth Warren are increasingly focused on. As you say, there's been an explosion of wealth inequality during the pandemic, much more so in the US than in Britain for example. Because the US stock market has gone up so much, in part because of low interest rates, and because the big tech companies are here in the US and their enormous success during the pandemic has driven up the stock market. There's also the inequality we write about in our book, which is the "inequality of respect," which in the US seems to come with education. To us, that's the deepest problem, because people without education have been left behind and are not politically represented.

What you say is exactly right, the major force today in international relations is what is happening *within* countries. That's exactly like what Martin Wolf said, that democracy is local, and globalization is global. The threats to globalization today are coming from *within* countries, not from *between* countries. We think it's the separation or leaving these people behind who favor populist solutions that are the real threat to globalization. If you get another decade of Mr. Trump, it's not clear how much will be left of globalization at the end of that.

Anne Case: Just to go back to what you said about NAFTA, speaking to some of the economists who were in the Clinton administration when NAFTA was passed, they knew that jobs would be lost in the US. But what they thought was that, well, this is a good time for the US to upskill, and so those jobs would be lost, but those workers would be retrained and that would lift everyone. But when NAFTA passed, the jobs were lost but the upskilling never took place, so those people were thrown out into the wilderness to fend for themselves. That's going to foment a lot of anger over a period of time as people feel like they're not participating when they see wealth increasing among some groups and they're not getting any part of that increase in the size of the pie. So that's a failure of policy and of democracy in the US.

Huiyao Wang: The US is home to around half of the world's top 100 universities and attracts talent from around the world, making it a very innovative country. I think this is probably the core strength of the US and China is learning from that. China has over 3000 universities and 35 million students on campus in total. So, education is certainly a key area China is paying a lot of attention to.

I would like to have David's comment on that as well. You've been living in China since 2016 and you are often contacted because of your studies on wages and labor economics. What's your take?

David Blair: There's a term that I hear in Chinese, one used for taxi drivers, anybody that operates equipment, or any sort of skilled job. Calling them "Shifu" is the way people show respect to a manual worker. A lot of these people are much poorer than people doing equivalent jobs in the US, but I don't think they feel the same sort of pressure and despair.

Some delivery workers, usually young guys from the countryside, work extremely hard with very long days and they may be under a lot of pressure from their employers to do things rapidly. But even for people working in places like parks, I don't feel like they think they are looked down upon. Whereas I think American working-class people now think they're just flat-out looked down upon, and that naturally stokes anger and a feeling of hopelessness. Do you think that's the right interpretation of what's going on?

Anne Case: Yes, absolutely. That's also something that separates the US from Europe. Go and travel in Europe, there's a lot of respect paid for people who do manual work that we don't see in the US.

Angus Deaton: But some of it is common with Britain, too. There is a new book, *Fulfillment*, about Amazon, [which describes how] people who used to work for Bethlehem Steel in Baltimore now work in Amazon warehouses. Where my grandfather died in a mining accident in Yorkshire, in that village where my father grew up, that coalmine is no longer there. The unions are no longer there. The solid Labour voters who used to vote for the Labour Party are not there, they're voting Conservative, and there's now an Amazon warehouse near the site where the mine was. Many people have written about how hard it is to work in an Amazon warehouse, in *Fulfillment*, but it is not dangerous like working in a mine, or dangerous like working in a steelworks was. These jobs are relatively well paid—Amazon is paying something like $15 an hour in the US. But there is a sense of despair that this is meaningless work, just working to the clock.

There are sociological accounts and individual accounts of these people's lives and there's a feeling that the meaning of life is not what it was back then and that there's been a lot of loss of society. For example, back then, Yorkshire mining towns had famous brass bands and famous soccer clubs; there was a social life built around those jobs, dangerous and dirty though they were. There's no similar social life built around an Amazon warehouse.

David Blair: That's the story that Robert Putnam [author of *Bowling Alone*] told for his hometown in Ohio, too. One thing that worries me is the next generation. Once one generation loses their jobs and the children don't get well cared for, or they may have psychological problems when they are young, how do we solve this problem for the next generation? Do you have any thoughts on that?

Anne Case: We are really worried about that too. If you've grown up and your mother is addicted to drugs or your father committed suicide, you don't have a stable home life, and the school that you attend isn't as good as the school would have been a generation ago because industry pulled out, the tax base imploded, and the school is not well funded. In this situation, your options for the future look pretty grim.

So, what do we do about this? This is a heavy lift, but we need to think about changing the educational system, which right now in America is laser-focused on the kids who are going to college. If you're going to high school but you're not college-bound, you're sort of on your own. We need to think about ways in which kids who are not going to go to university are going to get a skill set that's going to put them on a good career track where they could become skilled plumbers, or electricians, or learn to provide the different computer needs that we will have. We need to be thinking about how we make that happen, but that's going to be really difficult.

Angus Deaton: Actually, there is a lot of interest on both the right and left in the US in vocational education, of turning the educational system into something more like what they have in Germany. Also, to come back to the drum we like to beat, a lot of these local authorities are paying enormous sums of money for health care, and it's making it very hard for them to fund local schools, local education, and local universities.

David Blair: Just a point on China. There's a lot of interest around China in looking at the German apprenticeship system. But I still think there's too much attention, especially among parents, on forcing them to spend [very long hours studying] to get on the track for Tsinghua University or Peking University.

I'd like to follow up about the causes of this evolution in inequality. As I see, there are three major ideas out there. One is globalization—"let's blame Mexico," then "let's blame China," because it increases competition in the labor market and that has a negative effect. Another idea is that it is due to domestic policy changes. I notice there's a quote in your book which says that rent-seeking is a major cause of wage stagnation among working-class Americans and has much to do with the "deaths of despair." I'd like you to elaborate on that, and for the non-economists in the audience, explain what you mean by "rent-seeking." The third explanation is that it's just technological change and automation and there's nothing we can do about it. It could be a mix of those three things, but I'd like to know what you think the most important cause is.

Angus Deaton: Let's take globalization and technological change off the table. They exist and are very important; all countries face these changes in one way or another. But you're not getting the "deaths of despair" in most of Europe that we are getting in the US.

A few words about rent-seeking. What businesses should be doing is making stuff and selling stuff, as well as innovating, to get rich and make us all better off. That's a wonderful thing, it's what capitalism is good at, and what markets are good at. But there's another way that people can make money, which is that they can go to the government to get a special rule or regulation passed which makes them rich at the expense of everybody else, and that's rent seeking. Rent seeking is unproductive capitalism at its worst. The real danger in the story we're telling is that in many industries, including healthcare and banking, business interests have been very good at getting special regulations passed which protect them from market competition so that they can get rich at the expense of everybody else.

The story we tell, which some people agree with, and some people don't, is that in addition to the automation and globalization that is threatening the jobs of many working-class people in America, we've got rent-seeking, especially in the healthcare sector, which is twice as large as anywhere else in the world. China spends about 5 percent of its GDP on healthcare, the US spends 20 percent, and the median in Europe is around 10 percent. Yet other countries have a higher life expectancy than the US. America's healthcare industry is not "producing" more health, we have the worst health of any rich country in the world. Yet the business executives who run the hospitals, the device manufacturers, and especially the pharmaceutical companies are making enormous sums of money. The trouble is, that money can be used for further rent-seeking. The administration is trying very hard to undo some of these things. [US Secretary of the Treasury] Janet Yellen is a good friend of ours and has studied our book. Or Cecelia Rouse, our boss at Princeton and chair of the Council of Economic Advisers—they all know about this issue, but the politics is very difficult so it is a great challenge to tackle healthcare.

Anne Case: The hard part about the healthcare industry is, we don't think that this is a sector where you want the free market to work. Kenneth Arrow, who proved Adam Smith's theorems about how a market can work well, looked at the healthcare industry and determined that this was not a sector in which the necessary conditions hold for the market to work well. We shouldn't pretend that healthcare is an industry that can work well as a free market. The government will be needed to help organize what happens in the industry.

Angus Deaton: We understand the benefits of markets, we're not anti-market in any capacity at all. China really began to get rich when it deregulated markets and deregulated agricultural markets. We're all in favor of markets, but you need a muscular government to regulate the abuses that will happen if you don't.

Huiyao Wang: There are different forms of capitalism, such as casino capitalism, rentier capitalism, crony capitalism, democratic capitalism, and state capitalism. What is the ideal form of capitalism? China has a market economy in which the private sector accounts for about 65 percent, multinationals 15 percent, and state-owned enterprises around 20 percent. What is the best form of capitalism, and how can it be governed to serve the people well at the same time?

Angus Deaton: The struggle of people to make money is a very powerful force, what some people just call "greed." But it has to be channeled in ways that are socially productive. There's always a danger that greed will get out of hand and that danger exists in China, too.

Innovation is a big part of the story too, and something capitalism is very good at. In "creative destruction," new ideas come along and push aside old ideas, and people that were previously making money lose money, so there's a lot of churn going on. The danger is that people who become powerful from one set of innovations will try to stop the next round of innovation. That's not something specific to America, China, England, or anywhere. That's always going to happen and it's a danger in any system. You have to make sure that markets work for people and not just for the capitalists.

Anne Case: Part of that is if you want there to be evolution, there is creative destruction, and there are going to be people who lose. But those people need to be brought along too; if you want this evolution to happen peacefully, there needs to be a safety net for the people who lose out as innovation occurs. In the US, there was real pushback against helping people who lost out due to globalization or innovation. People were left on their own when these things occurred and their jobs disappeared. You can play the game that way, but it's not going to support a peaceful economic transition. I think we have to think about social safety nets as part of running a market system.

David Blair: I wanted to follow up with a couple of specific questions that China is dealing with right now. I went to graduate school in the late 1970s when the deregulation movement was in its heyday. People were arguing that you really don't need an active anti-trust policy, because the market will take care of things. And it was argued that you can deregulate the financial system because people can assess risk by themselves. China is now assessing where to go with both those issues, so I wonder if you could talk about them and whether you think they were a major cause of what's happened in the US economy over the last 40 years.

Angus Deaton: I think they were right then, but wrong now. Deregulation was not crazy, because regulations do generate a lot of rent-seeking. I knew American economist George Stigler when I was young, who noted that regulators were getting captured by the people they are supposed to regulate and that both sides joined together to exploit the people. So, there was a lot to be said for that deregulation and it generated a lot of growth in its time.

But in the situation now, I think there's widespread agreement that something needs to be done with the big tech companies, and how you regulate those while retaining the incredible benefits they've brought to us. I think China is struggling with that in exactly the same way now.

Those companies are very big and powerful and they're bringing huge benefits to us, but we're concerned about them and what they might do in the future.

David Blair: Tech is also more competitive in China. Alibaba is the equivalent of Amazon, but it has lots of competitors such as JD, while you really have Amazon by itself in the US.

Anne Case: With the financial markets and whether they can assess their own risk or not, and whether we can just let that roll forward without any oversight—I think we've seen what that led to in the US, which is people "lean into the wind" and then fall over, and ultimately the US government has to come in to shore them up because we can't let them fail. It's kind of a "heads we win, tails you lose" situation. I think it's kind of naive to think that the financial industry can just manage itself.

Angus Deaton: I agree with that. But again, deregulation in the 1970s wasn't entirely wrong. We got benefits from it, but it went too far. These things go through cycles. But something has to change, and I think both China and the US and everyone else is wrestling with that now.

One of the things that's happened in the US is that the countervailing power of democracy has weakened because rent-seekers heavily influence the government. If you go back to 1970, there was very little lobbying by firms in Washington. But lobbying has exploded over the past 50 years, and I don't think it's coincidental that that's the period over which the profit share has gone up and worker share has gone down.

China has a much more muscular government that tends to be more independent of interests such as industry or banking. That separation is very important, and democracy is supposed to be able to keep these interests separate, but it's not been doing it very well in the US. And not just in the US; there are a lot of people in Europe, with the development of populist movements and so on, who feel they are not well represented by parliaments that are dominated by people who have done well from globalization, people who are better educated and have little respect for their traditions or traditional ways of life.

Huiyao Wang: In terms of globalization, from which China benefits enormously, this year marks the 20th anniversary of China joining the WTO. What is your take on globalization? And if China rises peacefully, how can China, the US, and the EU work together toward greater economic prosperity?

Angus Deaton: I think we're in a really worrying situation where there's a real danger of "throwing out the baby with the bathwater." You could swing away from complete deregulation to a situation where there is total regulation and a stifling of everything. There's a lot of people in America who don't believe in capitalism in *any* form anymore. I don't think they're powerful enough to do huge damage, but they could be.

Anne Case: Regarding globalization, when you first study economics, you are taught that there are gains from trade, and indeed we've seen the pie getting bigger and bigger. But as the pie gets bigger and bigger, the question becomes, how does it get distributed—who "wins" or who benefits from globalization? In the US, too little attention was paid to distribution. A few people became very wealthy from this increase in the size of the pie that globalization brought. But a lot of people's lives were damaged, their communities were destroyed, and their families saw no prospects for the future, and no one took care of that. So, I think you need to make sure that things continue to work for the polity as a whole. If you don't pay attention to that, if you don't tend that garden, then bad things can happen, as we've seen happen in the US now.

Huiyao Wang: This has been a fascinating discussion. I think that the US and China, as the world's two largest economies, have a lot to learn from each other. You have offered a lot of valuable lessons and advice for us. So, to conclude, maybe each of you can say a few words on how these two countries can work together for a better future.

Anne Case: I think we need to look at the parts which are good and not throw those away. We need to work to build on these successes. I think a lot of the problems with globalization going as far as it has are *domestic* problems—about how we take the benefits of globalization and distribute them locally within our own countries. If we focus on that, I think we could make quite a lot of progress.

Angus Deaton: I think the big message of the last five or ten years is that countries need to put their own domestic house in order and not blame outsiders for what's happening. If they don't look after the people who've been left behind, which is a domestic policy issue, they run the risk of terrible things happening domestically, but also really bad things happening internationally. Because if people feel they are being exploited, they will look for scapegoats and they will blame anyone who happens to be around, whether it's China, or automation, or artificial intelligence. If you have a large fraction of your population whose life expectancy is falling, that's a domestic problem.

Huiyao Wang: That's sound advice and not only true for the US, but for China and other countries. We have to concentrate on domestic issues and handle our own situation well. Thank you, Professor Deaton and Professor Case for this fascinating discussion.

Angus Deaton and Anne Case: Thank you very much. Thank you, friends in China.

The Multilateral Trading System in a Changing Context

A Dialogue with Wendy Cutler and Pascal Lamy

Huiyao Wang, Wendy Cutler, and Pascal Lamy

On August 2, 2021, as part of the 7th China and Globalization Forum, CCG hosted a dialogue on trade between CCG President Huiyao Wang, Wendy Cutler, Vice President of the Asia Society Policy Institute, and Pascal Lamy, President of the Paris Peace Forum.

For this discussion on the multilateral trading system in a changing context, we were lucky to be joined by two good friends of CCG and leading authorities on international trade. Wendy Cutler spent nearly three decades as a diplomat and negotiator in the office of the US Trade Representative, where she served as Acting Deputy US Trade Representative. During this time, she worked on a range of bilateral, regional, and multilateral trade negotiations and initiatives, including the

H. Wang (✉)
Center for China and Globalization (CCG), Beijing, China

W. Cutler
Asia Society Policy Institute (ASPI), Washington, DC, USA

P. Lamy
Paris Peace Forum, Paris, France

© The Author(s) 2022
H. Wang and L. Miao (eds.), *Understanding Globalization,
Global Gaps, and Power Shifts in the 21st Century*,
https://doi.org/10.1007/978-981-19-3846-7_6

US–Korea Free Trade Agreement, the Trans-Pacific Partnership (TPP), US–China negotiations, and the WTO Financial Services Negotiations. She continues to be deeply involved in issues related to trade, innovation, and women's empowerment in Asia through her work with the Asia Society Policy Institute (ASPI). Cutler previously came to speak at CCG headquarters in Beijing in September 2018, participated in a joint CCG–ASPI roundtable on Asia's economic integration in March 2017, and also contributed an essay to the 2021 CCG book *Consensus or Conflict?* titled "Did the United States Miss Its Chance to Benefit from Ongoing Asia–Pacific Trade Agreements?".

Pascal Lamy was the longest-serving director-general of the World Trade Organization (WTO) so far from 2005 to 2013. Previously, he was EU Trade Commissioner, and before that, worked in a number of roles in the French government and as Chief of Staff to EU Commission President Jacques Delors. Pascal is now president of the Paris Peace Forum, which hosts an annual gathering of world leaders, experts, and individuals from around the globe to explore new forms of collective action. Lamy has visited CCG headquarters several times, including giving a talk on WTO reform in September 2019. I have also been fortunate to work with him through my involvement with the Paris Peace Forum.

In April 2021, a few months before this discussion took place, both Wendy Cutler and Pascal Lamy participated in a CCG webinar on the role of the WTO and the global response to the COVID-19 pandemic. Many things had changed by the time this dialogue took place, so we took the chance to review the impact of the pandemic and prospects for trade. This dialogue also took place in the run-up to the 12th WTO Ministerial Conference, which was later delayed, so the topic of WTO reform and related issues such as the dispute settlement mechanism, fisheries negotiations, and competitive neutrality were high on the agenda. We also covered vaccine inequality, the impact of China on the international trading system, regional economic integration, and global taxation. To start the conversation, Wendy began by giving us an overview of the Biden administration's trade policy.

Huiyao Wang: Let's begin our discussion today, and maybe I can start with Wendy. Since you are very familiar with the US government and a former US government official that worked on the WTO and multilateral trade for quite a long time, maybe you can start by commenting on the

US priorities for WTO reform and the upcoming 12th WTO Ministerial Conference.[1]

Wendy Cutler: Thank you very much. It's my honor to be here in another CCG forum. Before I talk about how I think the Biden administration is viewing WTO reform, the first thing is just to highlight three cornerstones of the Biden administration's trade policies, because I think that will help us understand their view on the multilateral approach, as well as on the upcoming WTO ministerial meeting.

First, the Biden administration's trade policy is closely integrated with its domestic agenda, including on issues like COVID recovery, climate change, and "Build Back Better." All these initiatives being pursued on the domestic front are also being pursued on an international basis. Second, when it comes to trade policy, the new phrase in Washington is a "worker-centric" trade policy. I get a lot of questions on what that actually means, so let me share some of my thoughts with you, but I would like to admit firstly, I think it's a "work in progress" and that how exactly this policy translates into concrete trade initiatives is still being developed. The basis for this policy is rethinking US trade policy as one that needs to change in order to benefit the working class and the middle class; to be responsive to their concerns and priorities; and to use trade to really improve, not only the number of jobs for US workers, but also to improve the quality of jobs, and again, not just US workers, but workers around the world. The phrase that [US Trade Representative] Ambassador Tai uses a lot is "to use trade as a force of good"—to really uplift the livelihoods of workers, as well as to promote more equality among workers, the middle class, et cetera.

The third pillar of the Biden trade policy is to work with allies and partners. We just launched, for example, the Trade and Technology Council with the European Union, which, for the purposes of today's discussion, includes a working group on global trade challenges. But it also is centered on being constructive and engaged in international organizations and multilateral institutions, including the WTO.

I think all three pillars are relevant to today's discussion. When it comes to the WTO, we did see some early moves by the Biden Administration to show that they are supporting the WTO, including very quick endorsement of the new Director-General, not even waiting for the confirmation

---

[1] At the time of this discussion, this meeting was scheduled for November 2021, but was later postponed due to COVID-19.

of Ambassador Tai. I'm sure we'll be talking more about Dr. Ngozi. Second, the US has been constructively engaged in the WTO agenda. Just last week, for example, we joined the plurilateral talks on services domestic regulation. We have been active members of the fisheries subsidies negotiations. And of course, we've joined ranks with others in calling for a Trade-Related Aspects of Intellectual Property Rights [TRIPS] waiver for COVID purposes. So, I think that gives some indication of how engaged and committed we are. That said, we still have not nominated nor confirmed an Ambassador to the WTO and lots of our statements on WTO reform have yet to be translated into actual proposals, but I think that will happen with time. However, I also think it's important that when we think about WTO reform and the upcoming WTO ministerial meeting, this can't just be about the US. This is going to require contributions from all 164 members, as well as the major trading countries, including Europe, China, and the US.

With respect to China, I think that it's going to be important for China to step up here and help move the WTO forward and update its rules. In particular, I want to highlight the WTO agenda with respect to non-market economies. This is an area, looking forward, where we will need to find a way to work together if the WTO is going to continue to be relevant. I think there will be a lot of interest in this agenda as we get closer to the 20th anniversary of China's accession to the WTO which will take place later this year.

The US has been very cautious yet realistic about its objectives for the upcoming ministerial meeting, partially taking into account where we are with COVID now and the possibility of in-person meetings. I also think it's important that we don't set high expectations and then not meet them. It's not in the WTO's interest for any headline around this Ministerial to use the word "fail" or not to have lived up to expectations, and so that's why the US has put forward what it calls a "targeted" approach, calling for a successful conclusion to the fishery subsidies negotiations, but also calling for some modest institutional reforms with respect to transparency, dealing with self-declaration developing country issues, and other institutional reforms.

Huiyao Wang: Great, I think you have highlighted the importance of the WTO. I'm very glad to see that the Biden administration is now backing the WTO. The new Director-General [Dr. Ngozi Okonjo-Iweala] has also appointed four deputy directors-general, one from the US, one from China, one from the EU, and one from Latin America. I agree that we should really focus on the future of the WTO because I think in light of this pandemic, we need world trade to reboot the global economy. In history, we have seen global trade boost stability and growth, such as after the Second World War and the financial crisis.

Pascal, you have been the longest-serving director-general of the WTO so far, you know the EU and China well, and you are a strong supporter of multilateralism. Biden has come back to multilateralism, the EU has always been there, and China is also a strong supporter of the multilateral system. So, what's your assessment? Can all the major players play a role to shape the revival of the WTO and to build confidence? Since the failure of the Doha Round, not much has been achieved.

Pascal Lamy: Short term, I think the main issue for all of us is to exit this pandemic—health-wise, economy-wise, and policy-wise. [The pandemic] is not mostly a trade issue, although open trade can help boost the recovery. There are a few [trade-related] issues that have to do with vaccine production and intellectual property, but these are not central to the multilateral trading system.

If we take a broader view, why do we need a multilateral trading system? Why do we need a World Trade Organization? Basically, to reduce obstacles to trade. In so far as a lot of us believe that open trade is a good thing overall, we need to reduce obstacles to trade. That is the big principle, which necessitates some qualification. I totally agree with what Wendy said, that the trade policy of the US, EU, or China is very much a domestic issue. The reason is that opening trade works overall to create efficiencies. If the sum of wins and losses is positive globally, there is greater efficiency, hence growth is higher. But this is usually not true locally and so the question is, what is the real impact of any country's trade opening on "x" profession, "y" group of workers, or "z" group of consumers. Well, this is something much more complex than the big picture.

In other words, while opening trade is a global issue and hence necessitates a multilateral trading system, a lot of attention has to be paid locally to how you manage distribution between winners and losers. There may be more winners than losers globally, but this may not be true locally. The reality is that in the West, for the last 10 or 15 years, there has been more debate about whether or not "we" will lose out in this equation, thus leading to more domestic political debates about trade.

That's a general introduction and the reality is that we have a relatively open world trading system that has worked for the last few decades. Trade is more open today than it was 10 years ago, and 10 years ago it was more open than 20 years ago. Yet, there remain a number of issues in terms of leveling the playing field, such as ensuring fair competition between producers so that the benefits of trade opening and competition can flow to the benefit of consumers.

In my view, in today's world, there are basically two substantive issues that need to be addressed multilaterally to level the playing field. One has to do with competition and another has to do with how you handle "precaution." Competition is about ensuring that producers compete on fair grounds, i.e., without trade distortions, which classically are quantitative restrictions, tariffs and subsidies. In today's world, quantitative restrictions and tariffs are not the major issues—they've largely been dealt with in the past—whereas subsidies remain a problem, notably because of China's role in the world economy. I think the main issue for the multilateral trading system and for the WTO as far as leveling the playing field is concerned is what the Chinese leadership calls "competitive neutrality."

The reality is that China has a different economic-political organization than the rest of the world, which is mostly organized in a form of global liberal market capitalism. China remains a communist country that believes that state control of 30 percent of the production system is the right way to go. This is very different from the rest of the world and it's probably more different now, at least for the last 10 years, than it was in the 10 years after China first joined the WTO.

"Competitive neutrality," how to compete in the Chinese domestic market and in international markets with state-owned enterprises (SOEs) that receive state support, is an issue that many other countries have to deal with. The EU and US probably are more outspoken than others in that they see this problem as one that necessitates further adjustment of WTO subsidy rules, but there are many other countries that have the same view. So, to ensure a level playing field and a fair system, I think issue number one is to strengthen WTO rules on state aid.

Another issue, which is more recent, has to do with what I call "precaution." Precaution is when you protect your people from risks, whereas protection is when you protect your producers from foreign competition. Precaution is now on the rise. It's about issues such as the environment, health, safety, security, and privacy. Precaution leads to more regulation and that regulation is more fragmented, because the way a state protects its people from risk is very often correlated with ideology, culture, religion, and history. This makes precaution a major, and tricky issue for the future.

There is another issue quite dear to my heart, but which unfortunately in my view does not get the level of attention that it should. It is that the WTO itself as a process, the way the organization works, needs a lot more attention and a lot of reform. As machinery to legislate and regulate globally, the WTO is not what it should be, for a number of reasons. I deeply believe that this machinery needs attention if we want the WTO to be up to its task in the future.

Huiyao Wang: Great, thank you Pascal. I think both you and Wendy have outlined your perspectives on the WTO and the future reshaping of the organization.

Pascal mentioned that SOEs play a large role in the Chinese economy, but they also have social responsibilities and play a frontline role in disaster relief and poverty alleviation. I think this hybrid system in China seems to be working, but you raised a good point about competitive neutrality, which is a concept being widely discussed in China. There is room for future improvement on this front.

I want to raise another question. Last year, both of you attended a CCG webinar on multilateral trading system reform, when we discussed the lack of leadership in the WTO at the time. Now, the US is back with the WTO under Biden, but we still need strong leadership to make progress, and cooperation between China, the EU, and the US. Wendy, you have recently suggested that we could have a US–EU–China forum on the multilateral trade system. Last time, we discussed that maybe the WTO Secretariat could play a more active role, like in the WHO and many other international organizations. In the WTO at present, with so many member states and rules, it's hard to make decisions. It would also be good to deliver on some low-hanging fruit, such as the ongoing talks on fishery subsidies. The WTO could also do more on issues like marine plastic pollution, digital economy and trade, and investment facilitation. Wendy, maybe you can share your views?

Wendy Cutler: Thank you. Maybe before I get to your question, just a couple of comments. I couldn't agree more with Pascal that we need to look at the WTO "machinery" and institutional issues because they are so interrelated in light of the inability of the WTO to produce successful negotiating outcomes. The approach that the WTO followed for its early years with respect to needing consensus to arrive at decisions, the focus on the most-favored-nation [MFN] principle under which all benefits from a negotiation should be applicable to all members, and the issue of LDC self-selection—are perhaps outdated now and they merit serious reconsideration.

You mentioned the fish subsidies negotiation. Well, one of the major stumbling blocks in that negotiation, from the US perspective at least, and of Europe and other countries, is that developing countries do not want to take on full obligations. I just want to make the link between these institutional issues, which sound very wonky, as they are so interrelated with where we see the WTO today. It's important that we look at these issues and, in my view, the only way forward is to allow for subsets of WTO members to meet, to negotiate, to agree on outcomes, and to share the benefits just among those parties, but at the same time to invite other parties to join and to offer them the technical assistance that might be needed to get them to a place where they can participate.

With respect to China's accession to the WTO, I am a firm believer that it was the right decision for the US at that time to be a supporter of China's WTO accession. When I look at the important legal and regulatory changes that China made at that time, how it opened and reformed its economy, and as you mentioned, how it became a global trade force, it has brought benefits to the international trading environment. I don't disagree with any of that. But I also feel strongly that here we are in 2021, and changes and updates need to be made if indeed this system can be credible and continue to function as a major force in the WTO rule-making process. When China joined the WTO, the expectation was that rules would be updated, there would be new market access commitments, and that we would continue to update the rules on subsidies or introduce rules on state-owned enterprises, among other issues areas. In fact, a new WTO negotiating round was launched that year. But we all know the history; none of that has happened. So here we are, and the status quo on these issues just doesn't work anymore. Looking ahead again, I think it's critical that China join others that want to see some changes in these rules to better reflect and govern the types of trade practices that China and some others are pursuing in 2021.

Now, with respect to your question, where can China, the US, the EU, and other major countries cooperate when we look at this WTO agenda? Where do our interests align? There are some areas. I think number one, fish subsidies is an area where we should be working together. It's critical that an agreement be reached on fish subsidies for the WTO's credibility.

This is going to almost be the litmus test for [Ministerial Conference 12]. If there's no fishery subsidies outcome, the headline is going to be "the WTO can no longer produce negotiated agreements." Moreover, we need to have an honest discussion about the special and differential exceptions [to the fishery subsidy rules], but we also need to make sure it's a meaningful agreement, that it doesn't just lock in the status quo. We should all be taking on obligations that actually address a real problem, and that is overfishing and over-subsidization, which have severe environmental impacts.

In the area of e-commerce we also have some shared interests. If we put aside some of the big issues where we have differences, like the free flow of data or data localization, there are areas with respect to trade facilitation and digital trade where we have shared interests, and maybe those are areas where we can work together.

On COVID recovery, I know there are differences between our governments, but I also think when you look at just the trade aspects, there are areas ripe for cooperation. The US now is in support of a TRIPS waiver for vaccines. I don't think this will be the end-all-be-all issue for COVID, it's just one part of the COVID response. But China supports this initiative as well, and I think we could work together with the authors of this initiative to try and limit it and make it workable, so we could have a meaningful outcome in this area.

Finally, I think it would be important for the multilateral trading system if the US and China could find a way to start taking baby steps toward lifting some of the tariffs that we have in place against each other's imports. Whether we could limit [the lifting of tariffs] to the medical sector, pick out some environmental products, or just reciprocally lift a small group of tariffs, I think that could be a real shot in the arm for the WTO going forward. We both know the history here—these tariffs are not helpful for either country, and it undermines the relevance and the credibility of the WTO if the two largest economies have such substantial trade barriers in place on each other's imports.

Huiyao Wang: Thank you, Wendy. I'm sure your last suggestion would be welcomed by the business community and would be a great move to show that both the US and China support the multilateral trading system and free trade.

Pascal, you spent so many years managing the WTO. What do you think about appellate body reforms, which have still not been fixed? Wendy also mentioned the TRIPS issue. To help overcome COVID-19,

China and the US need to agree to relax patent and intellectual property protections. Also, the EU has some proposals related to carbon issues. Perhaps you could comment on these issues.

Pascal Lamy: I generally very much agree with the points which Wendy has made. First, on this issue of China joining the WTO and the 20th anniversary of this accession. As you know, there's now a narrative in the West that suggests accepting China into the WTO was a mistake and that those who supported it, and I rank among them, were stupid enough to be cheated by China. This is absolutely wrong. I totally agree with what Henry said, you just have to look at the numbers. When China joined the WTO, its external trade surplus was around 10 percent of Gross National Product (GNP) and it's now around zero or 1 percent. How does such a change happen? There's only one way, which is to import more than you export, and this is what has happened. So, the answer is that China's accession to the WTO has been a big contribution to the world's economy.

Looking at the numbers, China's WTO accession has worked—that's not the problem. Where there is a problem we have to recognize is with the assumptions held 20 years ago when this deal was done. At the time, the assumption was that as time went by, over the long term, China would converge with the dominant global liberal market system. This did not happen, or more precisely, it did happen to a certain extent during roughly the first 10 years after China joined the WTO, and then in the next 10 years, China diverged from this path of convergence which started with Deng Xiaoping deciding China should rejoin the world economy.

I think the real problem with the WTO and China is that China professes exceptionalism as compared to global market capitalism, which then creates issues in terms of competition. This is why we need better, more precise rules on state aid. We Europeans know this problem—when the European common market was created in the 1950s, some of our economies were still more nationalized than others. Around 30 percent of France's economy was nationalized but only around 5 percent of Germany's. Under the deal done at the time, Germany said, I'm OK to open trade with France, but provided we have a system that regulates state aid, with a specific body which was the European Commission in charge of controlling whether or not state aid conferred an unfair competitive advantage. So, that's where we have an issue. It's not about China joining the WTO, it's about the fact that 20 years after China joined, China is more of an exception vis-à-vis the rest of the world than it was at the time.

I totally agree that there is a leadership issue. The solution to this leadership issue lies in adapting a principle, which is that the WTO is member-driven. "Member-driven" is one reason for poor leadership. Not that the WTO should not be member-driven at all. In my view, what should happen is what happens in other normal international organizations, which is a better balance between the authority of the members and the authority of the director-general and the secretariat. The current member-driven system should be changed to a system of "co-driving" the organization. On the one side, the members decide—not the director-general, not the secretariat. But the director-general and secretariat must be given the authority to make proposals, to identify issues, to look into options, like in any other international organization. This rebalancing is necessary—I think that the WTO would be much more efficient if the member-driven system was partially transformed into being more driven by the director-general. But at the end of the day, the member states will remain the legislature.

Looking forward, I agree with what Wendy said about the digital economy and fishery subsidies. It's now only a question of how to define exceptions—poor artisanal fishermen should not be subject to the rules. The question is, where is the line between artisanal and coastal fishing for poor fishermen, and large fisheries.

I see the environment as a major issue, in so far as climate change is now the number one issue on the international agenda. This necessitates urgent, bold action, which has to translate into an implicit or explicit carbon price rise. In the absence of a global agreement to set a global implicit or explicit carbon price at around €150, which is what economists say would be the right price to internalize the negative effects of production and CO_2 emissions, there needs to be different ways to address this problem tailored to different countries and constituencies.

As you mentioned, the EU has now embarked on a Carbon Border Adjustment Mechanism (CBAM). This is not a new musical instrument, contrary to how it sounds, but a carbon-border adjustment mechanism so that a high price of carbon in the EU does not lead to carbon leakage, i.e., EU producers moving production out of the European Union in order to benefit from a lower carbon price elsewhere. This is a major issue and a series of briefs by a Brussels based think tank called Europe Jacques Delors I have co-authored propose allowing countries to adopt different ways to increase the carbon price, whether it's through tax, emission permit exchanges, or regulations, and to compare the way they progress in order to smooth the inevitable trade frictions that differentiated carbon pricing in different countries will cause.

On TRIPS and COVID, I basically agree with what Wendy said. My own view is that there are already sanitary exceptions in the TRIPS agreement that provide for compulsory licensing in the case of a health emergency. We have a clear case of a health emergency, so what needs to be done is to make sure that the existing compulsory licensing systems work, as some think that they don't work quickly enough. It's not a question of overhauling the agreement, it's a question of looking at how these waivers as structured in the TRIPS agreement can be more quickly implemented, whether for domestic production or for imports.

Finally, on your question about the appellate body, there is a structural problem and there is a problem that is easier to fix. The structural problem takes us back to the issue of whether the WTO is able to adjust, to reform, and to adopt newly updated rules. As long as the rules remain as they were in the 1990s, you will always have a growing gap between reality and the old rules. It is the judges' job to adjust to this reality; old rules and new realities can only be reconciled within a dispute settlement system if judges interpret old rules so that they can match new realities. So, the real solution to fix the problem of whether or not the dispute settlement mechanism engages in judicial activism is to restart, reboot, and rework the rules-making system so that the gap between reality and rules is narrowed. That will leave much less room for judicial activism or "pretended" judicial activism.

The second part of the problem is probably not that difficult to fix. I believe the US is not always wrong when it criticizes the way that some WTO rules are sometimes interpreted. If the US would also raise this point about cases they win, it would be more convincing than the US only saying there's a problem when it loses cases. If you only criticize a judge when you lose cases and never when you win, it looks a bit strange. But let's leave that aside. There are, in my view, many ways to fix these problems if the US is willing to rejoin the dispute settlement system. By the way, the US is not the only country to believe that from time to time the judges may err in interpreting WTO rules.

This takes me to my final point, which I believe the three of us can agree on—that the key to fixing this problem is for the US, China, and the EU to work more closely together. The difference between the EU and China and the US is that it's not a fully fledged sovereignty. The EU's sovereignty depends on the topic, but trade is one area where the EU has authority, sovereignty, and size—like the US and China. I think this "G3" should work to fix a number of these problems—not that they should decide for others, but if there is a consensus between the US, China, and Europe, I would be surprised if it cannot translate into a WTO consensus.

Huiyao Wang: Thank you Pascal for your stimulating and forward-looking comments and recommendations. Now, I'd like to continue with Wendy if I may. You were the chief negotiator for TPP for many years, concluding talks a number of years before Trump pulled the US out of the agreement. There's a prevailing theory that the TPP was designed by the US to contain China as part of the "pivot to Asia." Now, China is interested in joining the CPTPP—not only China, but also the UK, Korea, and many other countries. What do you think about the CPTPP? There is also a trend toward regionalization, with RCEP, CPTPP, and other regional FTAs. How is that going to impact the WTO?

Wendy Cutler: If the WTO was actively engaged in rulemaking and delivering successful outcomes on important negotiating topics, the appetite for regional and bilateral trade agreements wouldn't be as high as it is now. So, the two are interrelated. The theory is that if you do bilateral and regional free trade agreements, those should provide momentum and push the WTO in the direction to do more, and that should contribute to liberalization. But it's not playing out that way. In my mind, if [over the next year] the WTO isn't successful in delivering some meaningful outcomes and getting itself back on the map, then you're going to see more and more trade move to regional and bilateral trade agreements.

With respect to TPP, all I can say is that when I worked on it, I would have never predicted we would be in the situation where we are now, where the US is out of TPP, Japan led other countries to conclude CPTPP, and now China seems to be more interested in joining CPTPP than the US. Sometimes my head spins when I think about all of this, but the story is not over either. It's interesting that with respect to TPP and the US, the debate has not gone away. In fact, some prominent senators, other congressmen, some noted foreign policy types in the administration, and others have been pretty vocal about underscoring the merits of a TPP-like approach and questioning Trump's decision for the US to exit the TPP. So, the debate continues, and if you carefully look at statements from the administration with respect to TPP, they are almost endorsing the approach of working with like-minded countries to set rules standards and norms, yet distancing themselves from the actual contents of what was in the TPP.

So, I don't think the debates are over in the US, but I'm also pragmatic and I'm a realist. I don't see a scenario in the near term where the Biden administration, given all that's on its plate and the domestic toxic nature of TPP, announces one day that we're going to rejoin. I don't see that happening in the near term. I think what's more likely is that the US works with other like-minded countries in the region to conclude a narrower sectoral type of deal, perhaps in the digital trade area, and perhaps that could build momentum for the US to participate in other negotiations in the region.

But I'm a firm believer that the US needs to get back in the trade space in the region, helping to shape the rules, the norms, and the standards. It's happening without us and we're not benefiting from it. When Trump left TPP, the feeling then was that the TPP would die a quiet death and that the RCEP would not proceed. But clearly, the opposite has happened; CPTPP is now in effect and the UK is formally in accession negotiations. RCEP will come into effect in early 2022, and it's going to have a real impact on trade, supply chains, and economic integration in the region. It's time for the US to get back into the trade game in the Asia–Pacific region, but this doesn't preclude our ability also to engage and lead in the WTO. The Biden administration has a lot on its plate, particularly with respect to COVID economic recovery, infrastructure, and competitiveness. But if we lose the opportunity to engage on trade in the region, it's something we might look back on as being a major mistake, and when we're ready to come back, it will be such a different Asia, and our ability to be a real player and to influence the rules, norms, and standards may be diminished.

Huiyao Wang: Thank you, Wendy, for your comment on that. I agree that the US needs to be back participating in trade agreements or even digital agreements. It's better than not coming back.

Pascal, you used to be the European Commissioner for Trade. At the end of 2020, China and the EU concluded in principle the negotiations on the Comprehensive Agreement on Investment, but progress has become bogged down again. Actually, European business is still very bullish on China. We have seen numbers coming from the EU Chamber of Commerce in China that European investment in China is increasing, with many European companies in the auto sector, pharmaceutical sector, or even aerospace now doing more business in China than in their own countries. How do you see prospects for China–EU business? Another question to you, as president of the Paris Peace Forum, which is a great multilateral global governance platform, to which you have dedicated much effort. How do you think the Paris Peace Forum can promote future globalization?

Pascal Lamy: Let me first come back to the point you made about China as a different system. I agree that those who thought 20 years ago that China would converge with the dominant system in the world, at least economically, were not right. The name of the game is not "convergence" anymore, it's about "coexistence." We have to better organize the coexistence of China with the rest of the system. It's not about regime change, it's not about the rest of the world telling China to change its doctrine or shrink its state-owned sector because a large state-owned sector would not be good for China, which I believe—that is for the Chinese to decide.

Whatever decision the Chinese leadership and people take on how they organize their economy, that is their business. But once the Chinese sovereignty decides that they want to have 30 percent of their economy under state control, because these companies are supported by the state, then you need to accept that others do not proceed in the same way, and that there has to be discipline on state aid to level the playing field. So, again, it's not about telling China how to run its business. Once China decides to have a massive part of its economy under Party and state control, this is a competitive disadvantage for others, which needs to be fixed. It's not a political issue, it's an issue of your own economy and the way you want to run it, but this should not put the others at a comparative disadvantage—hence the importance of "competitive neutrality," whether on the Chinese domestic market or when others compete with Chinese businesses in international markets.

On TPP, I very much agree that the TPP is the "best-in-class" for the moment. If you look at the most modern way to address both protectionism and "precautionism," TPP is the best benchmark on the market. The paradox is that it was a creation of the US; the whole software of the TPP is American software that coincides with the way the US sees the world, with the way the US sees manufacturing, service sectors, and intellectual property. TPP is very oriented to the US mindset and Australia, New Zealand, Japan, and others have accepted that. The paradox is that the US is now not part of this very US-oriented agreement, which is something of a mystery of history on which historians will probably comment 50 or 60 years from now.

I think that the way forward is probably that we do with CPTPP what we are doing with the WTO, that is, move away from the single under-taking and accept that TPP has bits and pieces, and that some of these bits and pieces can be joined by countries like the US, China, or the UK. I think this is the pragmatic way to go. CPTPP remains a leading agreement, especially if you compare it to RCEP, which is very much an old-style agreement that deals mostly with manufacturers, tariffs, and quantitative restrictions. RCEP is a large agreement, and hence it's impor-tant, but it's much shallower than CPTPP in terms of disciplines on how you run your economy in order to benefit from open trade.

As for the EU–China investment agreement, you're absolutely right that for the moment, this will not be ratified by the European Parlia-ment because of sanctions and retaliations about changes in Hong Kong or tensions elsewhere in China. So, let's be pragmatic on this. Nothing prevents China and the EU from effectively implementing this agreement without it being formally ratified, if we are serious about the fact that there are benefits for both sides. In this case it would not have been rati-fied, so it would not be legally binding as a treaty would be, but nothing prevents both sides from moving toward the content of this agreement in reality. I think this is the way to go.

On your last question about the Paris Peace Forum, it is not a trade forum and probably not fit to be a trade forum, because the Paris Peace Forum is about inventing new solutions, getting new projects done, about moving global cooperation into new areas with new stakeholders, whereas the multilateral trading system is much more about regulation. The Paris Peace Forum is about cooperation between non-state driven, non-sovereign partners like NGOs, businesses, big academic institutions, and big cities, and also with sovereigns, whereas trade is still regulated by sovereigns only.

What we can do is try to address the vaccine apartheid between North and South, which I personally believe is a dramatic problem that will slow our exit from this economic crisis, which stems from the sanitary crisis, by one or two more years. So, we are trying to work with the heads of the World Bank, IMF, WTO, and WHO through the Paris Peace Forum to promote cooperation, including trying to get through the next G20 commitments on more production and more distribution of existing non-used vaccines, which I believe is a major issue that we have to address quickly. I believe this new north–south fracture will divide this world and we will see the consequences of that in major negotiations, like talks on climate change for instance. So, I think this is a big problem. Not that trade issues are not important, but for the moment, there is something more important, which is vaccine production and distribution, which is a major economic and social issue.

Huiyao Wang: Thank you, Pascal, I congratulate you on your leadership of the Paris Peace Forum. I'm pleased that both Wendy and Pascal credit the CPTPP with setting higher standards for future global trade and maybe setting a good example for WTO reform. CCG has been advocating for China to join CPTPP, which is almost like a min-WTO. Since joining the WTO, China has abolished thousands of outdated rules and regulations, and that has helped to push China forward. We need some new targets to aim for and the CPPTPP could set a high standard for our future reforms as the WTO did in the past.

Pascal, the OECD recently proposed a global minimum corporation tax, which was also proposed by the G7 and G20. 130 countries have gone along with this initiative and China also agrees in principle. Then, there is the issue of digital tax and the EU asking big tech companies to pay tax. Maybe you can share the EU perspective.

Pascal Lamy: The issue of a global tax for multinational companies is one of the rare good news stories we've had in the last few years in terms of international cooperation. There are very, very few issues on which we can see progress in international cooperation. This is one and we owe it mostly to the Biden administration. Progress in this area simply stems from the importance and the growth of these multinational companies, including in the digital sector. They are making billions in profits without paying taxes and this has become unsustainable everywhere for political reasons. But to be frank, this breakthrough for international cooperation is an exception.

We need much more than this to reinvigorate international cooperation. I think the G20 is one forum to do that; not that it is a full-fledged institution, not that the G20 members have the legitimacy to speak for the rest of the world, but the G20 can be a place to forge much needed consensus on global public goods.

Huiyao Wang: Thank you. I really appreciate this discussion tonight, which was very stimulating, very constructive, and also full of ideas and suggestions. We have covered many issues: WTO reform, COVID-19, the future of multilateralism, even issues as concrete as TPP, fishery subsidies, and the Paris Peace Forum. So once again, I want to thank Wendy Cutler and Pascal Lamy, and our viewers. Thank you all very much and we hope to see you again sometime.

Bridging Differences Between China and the World

A Dialogue with Kerry Brown

Huiyao Wang and Kerry Brown

On March 2, 2021, CCG hosted a dialogue between CCG President Huiyao Wang and Kerry Brown, Professor of Chinese Studies and Director of the Lau Institute at King's College London.

Kerry Brown is one of the UK's leading experts on China. He has a long-standing relationship with the country, having lived in Inner Mongolia from 1994 to 1996 and later serving as the first secretary at the British Embassy in Beijing during his career as a diplomat with the British Foreign and Commonwealth Office. Since then, Brown has held a number of senior positions in think tanks and academia and written almost 20 books on modern Chinese politics. His most recent book, *China Through European Eyes: 800 Years of Cultural and Intellectual Encounter*, looks at how European thinkers through history have viewed and understood China in relation to their own societies.

H. Wang (✉)
Center for China and Globalization (CCG), Beijing, China

K. Brown
Lau China Institute, King's College London, London, UK

© The Author(s) 2022
H. Wang and L. Miao (eds.), *Understanding Globalization, Global Gaps, and Power Shifts in the 21st Century,*
https://doi.org/10.1007/978-981-19-3846-7_7

Before this dialogue, in November 2020, Kerry Brown joined a CCG webinar on globalization and China–Europe relations. He also contributed an essay to CCG's 2021 book *Consensus or Conflict?* titled "Forging a Partnership Between China and the World in an Era of Division: Finding Common Ground in Climate Change and Health."

Given Kerry's deep knowledge of China and his extensive research on external perceptions of the country, he was ideally placed to share insights on the gulf of misunderstanding between China and the West that seemed to widen as the pandemic unfolded. Our conversation, which took place soon after the inauguration of President Biden and just before China's annual Two Sessions and release of the 14th Five-Year Plan, covered factors shaping perceptions of China in the West, the challenges of understanding Chinese culture and history from the outside, and ways for China and the West to have a more productive dialogue. We started off our conversation by exploring Kerry's recent research into how European enlightenment thinkers viewed China and how many of these views persist today.

Huiyao Wang: It seems we are at a crossroads. In the last 10 days, President Xi has announced that China has realized the goal of alleviating extreme property, meaning that almost 800 million people have been lifted out of poverty. China is about to have its "Two Sessions"—the National People's Congress and the Chinese People's Political Consultative Conference (CPPCC). At the NPC, China is going to launch its 14th Five-Year Plan for 2021–2025.

We also see a lot of changes internationally. We have a new US president, President Biden, who will pursue quite different policies than President Trump. For example, on multilateralism, President Biden is very keen to cooperate on climate change and other issues such as addressing the pandemic and supporting the World Health Organization (WHO). We heard President Biden speak at the Munich Security Conference about 10 days ago, saying that while China is a competitor, there are also areas where the US can collaborate with China.

So, it is a time of new beginnings at the start of a new Lunar New Year. We'd love to hear your thoughts on some key topics that you've been contemplating for a number of years. I know that your recent book looks at how the rest of the world has viewed China across history, and in particular, how Europeans have perceived China in the past 800 years. We'd love to hear more about your forthcoming work.

Kerry Brown: It's an interesting time because normally each year I would go to China several times. In 2019, I was at the Schwartzman Scholars [at Tsinghua University] in October and November, went to see you and other partners, and I'd visit Shanghai and other places. For the last year, there's been none of that kind of physical traveling to and from China.

So, it means that we have to make an extra effort to maintain dialogue, particularly because politics never stops changing. Politics doesn't have to get on a plane and fly anywhere. Politics just happens wherever people are. Of course, the political context between China and the world has become much more complicated. Because of that, I started to wonder, has it always been that Europe and China have had a balanced but rather difficult relationship?

So, I went back further and kept on seeing quotes and works by great European thinkers like Leibniz, Montesquieu, Voltaire, Marx, Hegel, Max Weber, and Bertrand Russell, who actually went to China and lectured at Peking University in the early 1920s. And I went even further back to Matteo Ricci. I wondered whether there was kind of a "dual view" of China, sometimes really admiring China, sometimes really criticizing China. So, I pulled together the main works referring to China by the figures I just mentioned.

What struck me was that during the Enlightenment in the eighteenth and nineteenth centuries, particularly during the eighteenth century, many great figures wrote in some detail about China. This included figures like Rousseau—one of the most important philosophers Europe ever produced, a real polyglot, a man of incredible abilities across a whole range of disciplines; Montesquieu, whose work *The Spirit of the Laws* was so influential to the foundation of American democracy and the American Constitution; and Voltaire, the ultimate skeptical liberal thinker, someone who still is quoted and read today.

Although these thinkers hadn't been to China—of course, it wasn't easy to get there then—they did have a very distinctive view of the country. Voltaire was very admiring and made comparisons between Europe and China, such as comparing the Qing court and Qing emperor to the kind of systems that existed in Europe, and felt that China's secular system without a state religion was preferable. Leibniz was very much led by looking at evidence that came from China via the Jesuits. He was very close to many Jesuit scholars and read many of their works. He was really interested in what he called the Confucian system of governance. I really tried to look at what China presented to him. He wrote about how his position was not to make value judgments, but rather just to try to understand. In contrast, Montesquieu regarded China as a despotic and autocratic imperial system that was not at all attractive.

In a sense, these are three positions we still see today. It's extraordinary that some 350 years later these very entrenched positions are still there [...] European debate is divided between those who have a very critical view of China and regard China as a threat and those who are very admiring of China and what it's done with its economy and its political system—the kind of view that is not really that critical. And then there are the ones in that middle space, which is shrinking, who feel that we have a lot to understand before we can make big judgments. I suppose that's what universities are trying to do, but the politicization of universities has certainly increased and makes it more difficult.

I wrote [*China Through European Eyes*] because I wanted to know the historic roots of today. But today, I think it's more difficult than ever to have a reasonable debate about China or with Chinese colleagues that is not misinterpreted or framed as something that has some political meaning, either pro- or anti-China. If I study science, does it make any sense to say that I'm "pro" or "anti" science? I'm just studying science, right? My job as a Sinologist is to study China. There are many aspects of China—its culture, history, politics, and geography. I don't know what it means to say that I'm "pro" or "anti" China. I'm just interested in the facts that I see about China. I think that spirit is something we have to get back.

Huiyao Wang: Thank you, Kerry. *China Through European Eyes* is a fascinating book. It's good to go back to these historical views of China and see how much has evolved and changed. It will be very stimulating for people in China and around the world to look at China from a historical perspective, but also to take a realistic look at modern China.

As you have said, China is something of a hybrid. For example, in the Chinese economy, the private sector accounts for about 60–70 percent, state-owned enterprises make up another 10–20 percent, and another 10–20 percent comes from multinationals investing in China. This mix seems to work well in China.

You have written how China is a hybrid made up of many different elements such as Marxism, capitalism, socialism, and Confucianism. Historically, religion has not been particularly strong in China. In addition, the polity has tended to be rather centralized due to the need to deal with various challenges such as floods, irrigating vast territories, and dealing with invaders from the North. These factors have been important in shaping Chinese history and culture over 5000 years and remain important to the country's DNA today.

Next, what I would like to explore is how you see the gap between China and various different views of China around the world. Based on your observations, what do you think has contributed to this cognitive gap, and what could be improved or done to overcome it, both in China and in other countries?

Kerry Brown: I think that for Europeans and Americans, there are three things that are very new and very difficult to understand. The first is in modern history. I don't think there's ever been an appreciation of China as a strong and powerful country. Historically, since the nineteenth century, the era of colonization and the beginning of the humiliation of China, I think Western mindsets have tended to see China as a marginal place. China's role as an ally in the Second World War was never really appreciated; China's participation in the important post-war conferences was rather marginal, even though it had been one of the main allies for the Americans and British in the alliance against fascism. So, attaching this kind of marginality to China is in the European and American mindset.

Now, Europeans and Americans look at China—which has become much stronger economically, militarily, and politically—and the country is not marginal at all and is being restored to its place of historic importance. I think that digesting this shift is proving very difficult in the West as the attitude toward China that has been dominant for most of the post-war period is that it's a place that is separate and not really part of the developed world. Now, China is entering that developed world with one-fifth of the global population and a significant middle class. This is a big change and I think people are not used to thinking of China as a major equal power. That's the first problem.

The second issue is that we've never really thought of China as a global power. The consolidation of China's land borders historically and after the People's Republic of China was established in 1949 meant that China could be described as a land power. We've never really thought of China as a naval power but now we see that China has naval assets. I think China has more vessels than the US, though of course technologically, there are big differences. So, China now has power that can be projected way beyond its borders. It has a naval capacity and a cyber capacity. This is something new and I don't think we have really got used to this idea yet.

It has really occurred since the 1980s, with Admiral Liu Huaqing starting the process.

The third thing, which I think is the most difficult, is that the Western world has no idea of what it means to run a world or part of the world on "Chinese values." This clash of values is the most difficult to deal with because of two problems. One is that, while we think we are certain about our own values as Europeans or Americans, in the last few years, there's been confusion over what are our values actually are. We are divided in terms of our political values and when we talk about key terms like democracy, we often become more divided. Like the Trump presidency—does that represent true democracy or is it actually the opposite? There's no denying that people [in the West] are very committed to their beliefs, but these beliefs can vary significantly.

The second problem is that there is a lack of understanding of what to make of Chinese values. Either there is a desire to say that these values are not important, or there is simply no desire to understand them at all. I think that the West has often invested a lot into *not* wanting to understand China. It's like confirmation bias—you commit to a certain view, feel like you understand something, and no matter what evidence comes to you, you don't want to change your mind. We all do this about certain things.

I think that [in the West] there is an assumption that Chinese values are problematic and in conflict with the West, a threat to the West. I have argued, as have a lot of other people including Elizabeth Perry and other distinguished scholars, that Chinese values are "hybrid." Chinese culture and history have included many different kinds of ethical, philosophical, and religious views, from Confucianism to Daoism and contemporary belief systems. This has formed a very flexible worldview, one that I think is hard to immediately describe. I think that's really one of the problems; that in the current political environment in Europe and America, there is a desire to have a simple term, a simple label, that you can then embrace or attack. But I think China isn't a place that you can attach simple labels to.

There are some aspects of China, such as its work on poverty relief and climate change, that have been essential parts of a good dialogue with the rest of the world. There are other issues that have been much more problematic. So, it's not that there's complete agreement or disagreement. There is a broad range of complex issues that we take a different position on. I think it is difficult for people that have never really thought much about China or needed to understand the country, but now have to acquire this knowledge. For many of them, maybe there's not a desire to acquire this knowledge. They just want to have an opinion, and then, of course, their opinion is what guides them.

I suppose the job of my colleagues and I is to try to convey that China has this very complex world view, different belief systems, maybe different attitudes, and that we have to understand them before we can then see what the problem is. Some of those attitudes and beliefs are probably pretty unproblematic and some of them may be more difficult and will take a lot of dialogue. But we won't get very far if we don't have that dialogue. I think that's really what is lacking at the moment—a proper dialogue on what we do agree on and what we don't agree on, and then most importantly, what we do about that disagreement.

Huiyao Wang: On the question of power, for much of the last 200 years, China has been relatively weak. Now, it is rapidly rising as a global power, a land power, and a maritime power. With respect to values, some still expect China to converge with the West rather than accepting it is just different.

Deng Xiaoping famously said, "It doesn't matter if it's a white cat or black cat as long as it catches mice." I totally agree that China is a hybrid—we have market forces and elements of capitalism but we also have socialism with Chinese characteristics.

China has done many things right. President Xi recently announced that China has lifted 800 million people out of severe poverty. There are now around 1.3 billion people in the country that enjoy some kind of medical care coverage and over 1 billion people have some kind of social security, which probably makes China's welfare system the largest in the world. Now, people are forecasting that China's successful management of the pandemic will help to spur economic growth for many years to come. As scholars, both in and outside China, we need to examine what these trends mean for the future of the world. We should be willing to explore deep and complex questions, as things are not black and white.

Given that China contributes over one-third of global GDP growth, is the largest trading partner of 130 countries, and is a hub for global value chains, can China and the West find a way to peacefully coexist? Because otherwise, we're going to face a devastating conflict or end up in the Thucydides Trap, as my friend Graham Allison has said many times.

I'm encouraged by your commitment to deep thought and really digging into these issues surrounding China's rise in the world. In

Western foreign policy discussions, China is often described as a "challenge." But in one of your academic articles, you have written that the real challenge that China poses is one of "ontological complexity." What do you mean by that?

Kerry Brown: I think what is common in thinking and talking about China is complexity. When you are with an alliance, there are similarities to build on—a common language, common religion, or some common belief system—which give you a foundation from which to move to more complicated areas. But for much of history, Chinese dynasties from the Han onwards had only very limited relationships with Europe. Europe itself was not and is not unified, so it is quite a complicated situation.

Politicians face great pressures and they have to make things seem straightforward and simple. They have to come up with messages to convey something, like Trump's "Make America Great Again"—just four words. These messages get lots of people excited, even though you can argue about what they actually mean. But it is very hard to capture the China story in just a few words.

So, when I'm asked at events outside of China, how do I explain China and its rise in the world? It's something that takes a lot of explanation. China is not a capitalist country, but it uses elements of capitalism. It's a communist country, but one with a very specific form of communism shaped by the development of the communist party in China, which from the 1930s onwards was very distinctive under Mao Zedong. So, for many reasons, China is not an easy thing to convey in just a few words. You need an audience with quite a lot of knowledge. But many audiences don't have that knowledge because they haven't needed it until now. They may know some things about America, they may know some things about Europe, but they've never really had to think about China much because it's always been remote from them.

I think this is particularly true for the UK. Apart from Hong Kong, over the last century, the UK's historic links with China were mostly indirect. There hasn't really been a great deal of interaction and knowledge built up. In the 1960s, the Society for Anglo-Chinese Understanding was set up. [Its first chairman] Joseph Needham, a great scientific scholar, wrote *Science and Civilization in China*. I knew him very briefly at the end of the 1980s when I was a student at Keys [Gonville and Caius] College, Cambridge, where he was one of the fellows. But such figures were exceptional, they weren't part of the mainstream at all. In many ways, people could do most of the things they wanted without any real knowledge of China at all. When I was growing up, China was not part of my world. I remember in September 1976, the day when I saw this elderly Chinese man on TV and it was announced that the leader of China, Mao Zedong, had died. That was the first time I'd seen news about China on TV.

So, it's a dramatic change that now we have something like 150,000 Chinese students in universities in Britain. China is much more present. It's the largest trading partner of Australia and it's obviously a huge economic player. These things are all very new and happening very quickly. I think it was always going to be difficult to have a new player come along that appeared so quickly. On top of which, politically and culturally, this new player is very different to the ones that were dominant in the last 100–150 years.

There are three big differences [to deal with]: First, the new emergence of China as an important player. Second is China's political difference to America and Europe. The third is cultural difference. So, we need to have three kinds of knowledge, which is very difficult.

Many people say that Australia has worked out a strategy toward China. I don't think that is true. Australia has had extremely important economic links with China, there are 1.5 million Australians of Chinese heritage, and until recently, Australian universities had many Chinese students. But over the last 18 months, the relationship between Australia and China has really deteriorated. I'm not going to talk about whose fault that is, but I do think that Australia has some sensitive worries about its own identity. Is it an Asian country? Or is it just a European colony in Asia, which historically was the [main] idea and identity? I think those are really domestic issues and not so much about China, they're more about the identity of Australians, who they think they are and where they think they belong.

[These issues] were always there. They were there when Japan was a dominant economy in the 1980s. When I lived in Australia in the early 1990s, it was Japan that was regarded as the problem. And Indonesia because it is so close to Australia. So, it seems to me that China has become the third of these "worrying neighbors" that Australia thinks is a threat, not just because of economic and political issues but also because of identity issues. I think [identity and values] is where the dialogue about China becomes the most difficult. In terms of economic structure and politics, we can certainly identify areas of concern that call for tough dialogue with our partners in China. Trade negotiations were never easy, but we need to have them and we know where we're trying to get to.

What's worried me in the last year is that underneath a lot of these valid concerns, which we should and will talk about, there is something that is much more about identity. This idea of China being a threat because it's "not like us." When you ask, what does it mean to be "not like us," it creeps into areas such as China being ethnically or culturally different. [To some people it just seems] impossible for the world to have a dominant or even very prominent country that is not European or American.

The reason for this is not clearly economic and not clearly political. It's about something else. It may be a small minority of people that think this way, but I do think it is an area that we have to be very concerned about. In Australia, Britain, and America, [racial issues] have always been a problem in thinking about China, and Asia generally. There are valid concerns, but they get mixed up with these more racial issues, which have become more vociferous under the Trump presidency. There are expressions of opinions, which I find sometimes to be purely based on this idea of race, which I find repugnant. It's something that we have to condemn. But it's [an idea] that still enjoys some space, which is a huge worry.

Huiyao Wang: I think you've outlined a profound challenge that China is facing. China wants a peaceful rise, but the rest of the world, particularly those in the West, often lack understanding of China—as a different culture with a different history and a different system. It is difficult to reconcile traditional views of China with how things are changing rapidly and China's performance, especially economically.

So, it really falls to scholars, the think tank community, and policymakers to think about how we can have a new narrative to understand China. In China, we have a lot of work to do to develop a new narrative, but the same goes for the West.

China is developing so fast that it cannot be understood through a traditional lens. For example, China now has a billion smartphone users making their own decisions each day, such as where to go and what to buy, collectively forming a kind of "market democracy." With all this modern communications technology, China is not like it was in the old days when things were very autocratic. Now, the general public and the leadership are well informed and engage in a kind of consultative democracy. For example, the formulation of the 14th Five-Year Plan involved many layers of discussions and roundtables. As many as a million suggestions and comments were solicited and the plan will be discussed and revised again at the upcoming Two Sessions.

It's certainly a challenge to reconcile China's values with those of the rest of the world. But if China contributes to the prosperity and development of humankind, can we not be a bit more tolerant of different systems? It's clear we are not at the "end of history." So, I think it is crucial that scholars from China and around the world can engage in more discussion and dialogue.

I know that from 1998 to 2005 you worked at the British Foreign and Commonwealth Office as a diplomat, serving as first secretary at the British Embassy in Beijing. You also lived in the Inner Mongolia region of China from 1994 to 1996. So, you are truly a "China hand." With your experience as a diplomat, scholar, and think tanker, how do see the challenge we have now? What gaps of understanding do you see, particularly in the area of foreign policy, between scholars in China and in the West? And how can we overcome these differences?

Kerry Brown: I guess there are two ways of acquiring knowledge. One is deliberately and the other is by accident. If I've gained knowledge about China, it's been probably more by accident than design. I didn't do Chinese as a student at Cambridge, I did English literature. I later developed interests in China, actually while living in Japan in 1991. I visited China, went to Beijing for a week and really felt, "wow, I want to know more about this place." After that, I really concentrated on understanding the Chinese language and history, more modern history than imperial history. Since then, I've read as much as I could about the long narrative of Chinese history.

I guess the easy thing to say about improving the current situation is to say "education." We need to have more education, certainly in British schools, about Chinese civilization and Chinese history. We need to have more people studying Chinese. We need to make China familiar. But the outcomes of this will probably be very difficult to assess—just because you know more about something or somewhere, doesn't mean you're going to have a better attitude toward it. After all, British views toward Europe are very complicated, and we know much more about Europe than we do about China. People may study French, German, or Italian at school, but it doesn't necessarily mean they will have a very friendly view [of these countries]. They may end up having a less friendly view. So, we can't just assume that education is going to be a perfect medicine.

I think it's going to be a long period of adjustment. I don't really think that the Thucydides Trap is the issue, this is a unique situation that we've never had before. America and China are two nuclear powers that will not use their ultimate weapons against each other, because that would mean mutual destruction. That really restrains what they can do to each other.

The second problem is that, unlike the Soviet Union, China is in some ways a capitalist actor. Its economy has strong elements that seem very similar to capitalism and it's integrated into global finance and supply chains. For all the talk about decoupling, it is unlikely to happen. The attractiveness of the Chinese domestic market is going to be a very big incentive for companies, wherever they are from, to engage with China. We saw this last year with the drafting of an investment agreement between Europe and China. While Europe is increasingly arguing with China about human rights and other issues, it's also agreeing on the framework for an investment agreement. There is an immediate conflict between what Europeans want; they want one thing [from China] but not the other, and they can't pick them apart.

When you look at the complexity of these problems, I think the most you can say is that the worst outcome is unlikely—thankfully. It's likely that issues like climate change are going to get more serious and so the pressure for China, Europe, and America to work together will get greater, out of self-interest, and that gives a pathway to find ways we can work together for the common good.

I also think that we are going to have to construct a language of disagreement so that for any argument, no one walks away with a complete victory, and no one walks away in complete defeat, or at least not often. Usually, it isn't good for either side to be completely defeated, as they'll likely be very resentful. What you want is an exchange. There are ways in which partners can talk to each other. We do this all the time—as people, as communities, and as institutions. We have dialogue, we agree, we disagree, and we reach some kind of midpoint. With China, that's going to be a multi-layered discussion. We're a long way into this discussion, but we've still got a long way to go.

What we're looking for is a framework under which we can agree to disagree, I think that's the important thing. The strange thing is, I think we are clear about where we can agree—we can agree on things like climate change, how to deal with global health issues, and sustainability. There's a consensus, so with China, we're dealing with a partner on those issues—and these are the big issues for human survival. But we're going to need a way to deal with disagreements, which may be significant, but they are not to be important enough to jeopardize the future of humanity. [After all,] what could be more important than that?

I think this is the stage we're in and it's going to be a long stage, it won't be sorted out easily. Henry, that means you and I are in a growing sector because there will be a golden age of diplomacy and dialogue. That's good, but it doesn't mean the dialogue will be easy. I think we just have to accept that. We shouldn't try and accelerate things too much; we just have to deal with our disagreements step by step.

Huiyao Wang: You've really hit on some of the challenges that we are facing. I agree that we need more dialogue. Trying to really understand each other is a daunting task for scholars like us. For the international community watching a rapidly developing China, the question of how we can shape a new understanding and narrative while being able to agree to disagree is a key question. I hope we can talk and seek common ground despite our differences, as captured in the Chinese saying *qiu tong cun yi.*

Moving on to geopolitics and international relations, in President Biden's speech to the 2021 Virtual Munich Security Conference, he spoke of the need to prepare for "strategic competition" with China. He didn't use the word "rivalry" as President Trump had in the past. He described many challenges linked to China, but also areas like climate change and the pandemic where we can work together.

On the same day at the G7 summit, I was glad to see that President Biden pledged $2 billion of funding to support developing countries in fighting the pandemic, a similar pledge to that which President Xi made in May 2020. The two leaders also had a long telephone conversation on Chinese New Year's Eve, so there seems to be some positive progress. How do you see the future of Sino-US relations, will trade remain a contentious issue? Will the US seek more to forge a Western alliance? At the Munich conference, I noticed that Chancellor Merkel and President Macron were not completely aligned with President Biden. Merkel said that we have to deal with but also work with China. President Macron stressed that strategically, the EU will be more independent as the US focuses more on the Indo-Pacific.

Recently, I noticed a report by the US Chamber of Commerce which said that the trade war could cost the US 1 percent of GDP and several hundred thousand jobs. So, what do you see for the next four years of this Biden administration? Economically, will they continue Trump's policies? Politically, will there be a shift toward alliance-building? Because in terms of alliance-building, countries such as members of ASEAN may prefer not to take sides. Prime Minister of Singapore Lee Hsien Loong has said that they don't want to take sides in containing China. How can we repair Sino-US relations so they become more constructive?

Kerry Brown: The tone of the new American president, compared to the previous one, is different and that will help. Often, the provocative and aggressive language Trump used created its own problems. The second thing, which is maybe underappreciated, is that Trump didn't really delegate properly. He didn't build a [proper] team around him and it was very unstable—it was really all about him deciding everything. Biden has a very competent team around him, like Secretary of State Blinken and others that are very experienced and capable. It seems that there will be much more of a team ethos, which should be helpful.

The third thing is that, although Europe and America are not going to be completely aligned, I think they are now speaking more to each other about China and working out their common points. That will probably be helpful because I think it's good for America to realize that it cannot really promote a China policy on its own, it needs allies. That means that there will be more multilateralism and probably some of the more extreme ideas of the Trump era will disappear, there will be more moderation and nuance.

Fundamentally, the issue is most serious for America because it is currently the world's biggest economy and China is competing with that. Psychologically, this is a huge moment; there will be a day, sometime in the next five to ten years, probably sooner rather than later, where we will wake up one morning and China will be the world's biggest economy. This will be a historic moment—the first time in modern history that an Asian country has been number one, the first time in modern history when China has been economically number one, the first time in history when a Communist country has been number one. Symbolically, it will be incredibly difficult for America to know that they're going to be number two, economically. Of course, in many other areas, they won't be number two—militarily, or in terms of their alliances, they will still be number one. But I think it's going to really have an impact on how they view themselves and their status is in the world. This will be a problem. America has a sense of self-esteem and pride, and because they will no longer economically be in the number one position, I think this will then feed a lot of other doubts.

For many years, we've wondered whether America is a declining power, and many times, we have [recognized] that it is still dominant in many areas, from economics to technology. The world's biggest companies are mostly American. Military, if you add up the top five [nations after America] they are still not equal to America's [military expenditure]. The US is still the most powerful country and is likely to be so for a long time.

However, this one indicator—[the decline of] America's economic status—will be symptomatic of a larger shift and is feeding a lot of the anxiety in America. It's not just about economic change, it will then mean a whole bunch of other changes. In effect, America will no longer be the richest country in the world. Sure, per capita [GDP] is totally different. China is still a middle-income country, basically a "moderately prosperous" country in per capita terms. But in total, China will be the richest country in the world, and this will be one of the key geopolitical moments of modern history, probably more significant than the collapse of the Soviet Union, probably more significant than any event since the Second World War.

It's already starting to have an impact. China's economic growth has been greater than America's coming out of the pandemic. Every day [China] is getting closer to that target of [US total GDP]. I think when China is even closer to that target, there will be more political turbulence. When Japan was around two-thirds the size of the American economy in the late 1980s, there was already anxiety over how to deal with Japan. That problem passed and I think there's a hope in America that the same will happen in China, that there will be some issue and China's growth will fall, but at the moment we don't see that. The pandemic has had some impact but the IMF forecasts that at least this year, China's economy is likely to grow and continue to grow well. So, unless there is a total disaster, then I think that China is on this path to become the dominant economy, and the political implications of that are very profound.

Huiyao Wang: I think you've given a very accurate analysis of what we're going to see in the next five to ten years. China is rising rapidly, both economically and politically, so how can the world, particularly the US, accept that? As you said, the US has been in the number one position for a hundred years now. But now, China has emerged and is poised to overtake the US to become the largest economy in the world. Psychologically, it will take a while probably to adjust.

At the same time, we also live in a world of shared challenges, such as overcoming the pandemic, that call for China, the US, the EU, and all other countries to work together. President Biden is committed to tackling climate change and needs to collaborate with China on that issue. Hopefully, as new risks and challenges emerge, our common interests can help unite humankind. I hope that we can set aside ideological differences and some of the biased views we hold toward each other and work on tackling the common threats we face.

After the Second World War, as the US forged a new international order, [in 1944] we had a "Bretton Woods moment" as we built the new system. Maybe the pandemic can spur a new "Bretton Woods moment" so that we can enhance global governance and the delivery of global public goods, addressing questions such as how we can fight future pandemics, or whether we can build some kind of global climate organization. Another key area is infrastructure, which is lacking in many countries, even the US. Could we, for example, upgrade the Asian Infrastructure Investment Bank into a "World Infrastructure Investment Bank" through which China and the US could work together, along with the World Bank and other multilateral development banks? There is also scope for China and the US to work together through the Belt and Road to spur an infrastructure revolution to modernize the whole world. There are many common things to work on rather than fighting each other.

Moving on to Europe, which is in a unique position. How do you see China and the EU, which recently concluded the negotiation on the Comprehensive Agreement on Investment with China? Commercial ties are important and China is the EU's largest trading partner. Could the EU, which is an important ally of the US, play some kind of mediating role in China–US relations, such as participating in a trilateral summit between the EU, the US, and China. The EU shares many interests and a long history with the US but also has deep business ties with China. How do you see the new investment treaty and the future role of the EU with regards to China and the US?

Kerry Brown: One of the strange things is that in recent years, the EU, China, and America haven't had a formal trilateral dialogue. They never really sit down with each other and talk about common issues; they may do it as part of the G20 or other forums, but as three separate entities, they don't sit down and talk together.

Part of that is because I think that the Chinese and the Americans are very jealous of their relationship. They don't want others to come in, they are the two great powers, so they are quite protective. I think the second reason is that the European Union has 27 member states. It is different to America and China, not a single sovereign entity but rather a kind of consortium. With the British leaving the European Union, which was unfortunate, we now see Europe consolidating again. For a while, it looked like Europe was really threatened as a project. [The EU] goes through ups and downs and is perpetually in crisis in a way, but you have to acknowledge that this consortium is helpful and does deal with some issues well. Investment protocols are probably one such issue. [The EU] is a good way to negotiate because of the size of the European investment and trade market.

If Europe, China, and America could talk to each other, it would be a very important global gathering. The EU and China have a high-level dialogue, China and the US have high-level exchanges, and the Europeans and the Americans have a dialogue on China. So, the one thing that's missing is that they all get together. Is that possible? For issues like climate change and pandemics, it makes a lot of sense. Whether they'll be able to find common cause is another matter. I think America still feels that it should be in charge of the relationship with China. It doesn't mind if Europe agrees, but [the US] doesn't like it so much when Europe disagrees [on China]. For China, I think there is a sense that [taking part in such a trilateral summit] would mean going into a meeting with two other participants that are against it. So, I don't think that we're quite at the moment where [China, the EU, and the US] will sit down together. On climate change there is common alignment; Biden has brought America back into the Paris agreement, Europe is committing to decarbonizing its economies, and China has committed to becoming carbon neutral before 2060.

I think these [climate] targets will become more ambitious and so this is a large area of potential collaboration. If America, Europe, and China agree on something in this area, it will have a huge impact—especially if you can bring India into it, then you've already covered a vast part of the world in terms of population, geography, and economy. Once that is in place, then others will likely follow. The potential leadership role of China, the EU, and the US is huge. I'm hopeful that [climate is an area] where real dialogue and collaboration with China can happen, which could lead to very beneficial outcomes for everyone.

Huiyao Wang: In the last two years, CCG has proposed the idea of a trilateral dialogue between China, the EU, and the US at the Munich Security Conference, particularly while China and the US have been locked in a fierce trade war and there are also tensions around issues such as the Taiwan Strait, South China Sea, and sanctions. When two large players quarrel, it is helpful to have a third party that can mediate and calm the situation. But instead, after this suggestion was made, actually, the EU and the US set up a dialogue on China without China participating.

I agree that we really need the US, China, and the EU to work together on issues like climate change and the pandemic. CCG has also suggested establishing a climate summit including the G7 members as well as China, India, and Russia. Together, these members would account for over half of the world population and include the six biggest carbon emitters. Somehow, we need to engineer a new Bretton Woods moment for our post-pandemic era, to forge new mechanisms. Existing institutions such as the G20 and United Nations are great, but we also need more focused and specialized institutions.

Since you are in the UK and live in London, I want to raise a question about Brexit. The UK has now separated from the EU but has also applied to join the Comprehensive Trans-Pacific Partnership (CPTPP). The UK still has a lot of influence and soft power. Joining the CPTPP and working more closely with China would allow the UK to look beyond the EU and realize the vision of a "Global Britain." What do you think about the state of China–UK relations, particularly now there are a lot of disputes over issues like Hong Kong? Is it possible to reconcile these differences or even get back to the "Golden Age" of China–UK relations? As you said, the UK is the second-largest destination for Chinese students, with over 150,000–200,000 students studying in the UK, as well as tourism and many other areas of cooperation. So, what can be done to improve relations and what do you think about UK's new role regarding cooperation with China, now and in the future?

Kerry Brown: It's been a difficult year because of COVID-19 and an increasingly political fight. Part of the reason is that I think historically, when the Conservative Party has been in power, they have been maybe more confrontational with China, at least according to what I remember. Now they are the dominant party and there is a significant group within the Conservative Party that has created an organization called the China Research Group. They clearly see China as a very particular kind of problem and are keen to make that the way that we understand China–UK relations.

As I've said, historically, on the whole, China has not had a high-profile image in the UK, it's been more marginal. Britain has not paid that much attention to China; its main interests have been in Europe and America.

So, there's a lack of understanding about what China is and what China should mean. Now, we have a lot of people who do talk about China, but mostly this is within the framework of COVID-19 and the political issues, such as where [the virus] came from, how it happened, and who is to blame. This has distorted the discussion on China in the UK and people have lost sight of the longer-term issues.

Many people now talking about China never had much of an opinion about it before, because it now suits their particular political interests. The populist politician Nigel Farage has suddenly started taking note of China. He is a nationalistic figure and was one of the main influences behind Britain leaving the European Union. I think that's unfortunate; once someone with his kind of track record—of creating problems, divisions, resentment, and manipulation—becomes interested in an issue, it usually makes public debate more difficult. Despite that, I think that British people are pragmatic and there will be many opportunities to find spaces to work together. I think that we are more moderate in our approach.

We have many people trying to influence us now. Strange, slightly worrying figures like Clive Hamilton, an Australian academic who's been making big claims about how China influences politics in the world. I think this kind of language does have some influence in the UK. But there are also voices that are more moderate and thoughtful. When I talk to politicians, I'm struck by the fact that while they may say one thing in public, in private, they are aware of the complexity of what they're looking at, and they're trying to find a road via which we can look after our interests despite the disagreements. I think we're all trying to find that middle road; to look after our interests and acknowledge that we need to cooperate in certain key areas, [while also accepting] that there are other areas where we won't be able to see eye to eye.

I think [British] politicians have not gone to the extremes of some in Australia or America. So far, there's no very prominent public figure signed up to the idea of a huge "China threat." But the issue is still developing and it's something that we shouldn't be complacent about. For my work, I'm not here to "convert" anyone. I just want to have the best possible debate about issues around China, the best understanding of what we think about China and what China means to the UK. I'm optimistic because in most surveys it seems that moderates and those who are more pragmatic outnumber those with more [extreme views].

I'm not saying that there aren't things that we should be concerned about and that we should really focus on. But I do think that we need to be pragmatic. That's something we can learn from the Chinese because I think in the last few decades the Chinese also have been pragmatic, and it seems to have worked in some areas for China. I hope that pragmatism can also work for us.

Huiyao Wang: Thanks, Kerry. A lot of our discussion has centered on the gap between China and the outside world and how to minimize it. But there are also significant gaps within countries. For example, in the US, the widening gap between rich and poor has contributed to the rise of populism and the election of President Trump. China also has issues with inequality, but the government has mobilized to eliminate extreme poverty and last week announced that nearly 100 million people have been lifted out of poverty in the last eight years.

In the US, President Biden wants to raise the minimum wage from $7.8 to 15 to help address poverty in the US. Sometimes, China is made a scapegoat for issues related to income inequality in the US. For example, some say that everything is now "Made in China." But that doesn't mean that China reaps all the profit from these goods. Actually, multinational corporations account for 40–50 percent of Chinese exports. For an Apple phone that sells for $1000 in the US, China makes maybe $50. In the last few decades, multinational corporations have made huge profits but probably haven't made sufficient contributions to their home or host countries. More international cooperation is needed to build a form of global governance that ensures globalization can benefit all countries. This would probably help to quell populism in various parts of the world. What is your view of these issues?

Kerry Brown: I think China's achievements in poverty alleviation should be better appreciated in the outside world […] In the last 40 years, a huge number of people have been lifted out of poverty in China. Whatever the reasons for that, it's an achievement. I think we need to recognize that. This is why China is not a straightforward story. For all the things that people are very critical about, things that you should be critical about, there are also some things which are huge achievements that should be celebrated. Yet it's not easy to say that sometimes because the narrative is always very negative, and you don't get much coverage of those things which are much more positive.

What strikes me is that China's achievements are something we can all learn from. One simple answer [to your question] is that we need to have a forum for learning, not just for dialogue but for learning, which is a two-way process. One mindset is that it's always been America or Europe going to China to teach and to show how you do things. I think we now need some recognition that there are many issues on which China can teach the rest of the world and show how to do things. Building high-speed railways has been one huge achievement. Poverty alleviation is another. There's green technology and various innovations in other areas. There are some areas where [this mutual learning process] won't be possible, but there are other areas where I think we must learn from each other. The era of the "great learning" should start and it shouldn't just be one way. It should be learning from people who have something to teach, and that includes China.

Power Shifts and Great Power Relations

Power Shifts in the Twenty-First Century

A Dialogue with Joseph S. Nye Jr.

Huiyao Wang and Joseph S. Nye Jr.

On April 28, 2021, CCG hosted a dialogue between CCG President Huiyao Wang and Joseph S. Nye Jr., Harvard University Distinguished Service Professor, Emeritus.

Joseph S. Nye Jr. is one of the world's leading scholars in the field of international relations. His work has explored various notions of power and he is famous for developing the concept of "soft power." In addition to his long and distinguished career at Harvard, which included serving as Dean of the Kennedy School of Government, Nye has also held several posts in the US government, including Assistant Secretary of Defense for International Security Affairs, Chair of the National Intelligence Council, and Deputy Under Secretary of State for Security Assistance, Science and Technology. Nye has published a number of influential books, the most recent of which include *Soft Power, The Powers to Lead, The Future of Power, Is the American Century Over?,* and *Do Morals Matter? Presidents and Foreign Policy from FDR to Trump.*

H. Wang (✉)
Center for China and Globalization (CCG), Beijing, China

J. S. Nye Jr.
Harvard Kennedy School, Cambridge, MA, USA

© The Author(s) 2022
H. Wang and L. Miao (eds.), *Understanding Globalization,
Global Gaps, and Power Shifts in the 21st Century,*
https://doi.org/10.1007/978-981-19-3846-7_8

I had the pleasure of getting to know Joseph over a decade ago during my time at the Harvard Kennedy School of Government. Since then, I have enjoyed several discussions with him, including a virtual roundtable as part of the State of Europe event hosted by the Brussels-based think tank Friends of Europe in October 2020. Joseph also contributed an essay to the 2021 CCG book *Consensus or Conflict?* titled "China and the United States: Looking Forward 40 Years."

Our discussion centered on great power competition and prospects for China–US relations. Nye started off by describing two global power shifts that will shape the twenty-first century. The first is a "horizontal" power shift from west to east. The second is a "vertical" power shift from governments to transnational and non-governmental actors. We went on to discuss topics such as soft power, the importance of "social interdependence" in promoting understanding between different countries, and the relevance of historical analogies from the twentieth century to current geopolitical tensions.

Huiyao Wang: Your most recent book, *Do Morals Matter? Presidents and Foreign Policy from FDR to Trump* explores many dimensions and CITIC Publishing House is looking forward to publishing it in China. This is a good theme to open our dialogue today.

Joseph S. Nye Jr.: I think the topic of how power is changing in the world and how that's going to affect relations between the US and China is one of the absolute central topics of our century. In the last chapter of *Do Morals Matter?* I say that there are two great power shifts going on in this century. One is a power shift from west to east, which means from basically Europe and the Atlantic to the Pacific and Asia. If you think about the world in, let's say in 1800, Asia was half of the world's population and half of the world's economy. By 1900, Asia is still half the world's population, but only 20 percent of the world's economy because of the industrial revolution in Europe and North America. What we're seeing in this century is a return to normality, normal proportions. It's a long process, but I think it's an extraordinarily important power shift.

Many people see this as the rise of China and certainly, China has been central to it. But also, it starts really with the rise of Japan after the Meiji Restoration, continued also with the rise of India. So, China's a big part of Asia, but Asia obviously is a broader concept. So, how do we manage that power transition from the west to east in a way which is beneficial for all countries and which doesn't break down into great power rivalries, which are destructive? That is one of the great power shifts.

The other great power shift is what I would call "vertical" rather than horizontal. That's the power shift from governments to non-governmental and transnational actors. This is driven by technology and by changes in not economic, but in ecological globalization. Things like pandemics and climate change, which don't respect boundaries and which no government can control working alone, [things that have to] be controlled by working with other governments. That's why in my book, I talk about the fact that the first type of power shift, the one that I would call horizontal, is one that can lead to "power over"—competitive power, in which we think in traditional terms of "power over" other countries. When you look at this other power shift, the vertical one from governments to transnational, this requires a different form of power, called "power with" rather than "power over," because no country can solve those problems alone. So, if you take climate change, for example, China cannot solve climate change by itself. The US can't solve it by itself. Europe can't solve it. It's going to have to be cooperative, yet it's tremendously important for each of us. If the Himalayan glaciers melt, that's going to destroy agriculture in China. If the sea levels rise, that's going to put much of Florida underwater. Neither [the US or China] can deal with that acting alone, we have to work with each other. That's the importance of "power with."

So, what I argue in [*Do Morals Matter?*] is that these two power shifts lead to an emphasis on two different types of power, "power over" others and "power with" others. If we're going to have to learn to live in a world where we manage both simultaneously, that's not easy. People always like things to be simple—either one or the other. In fact, it's going to be both.

Huiyao Wang: Thank you, Joseph. I think you illustrate well the power shifts occurring and the nature of horizontal power "over" and vertical power "with."

You are an authority on power narratives, particularly soft power. You first coined the term "soft power" in your 1990 book *Bound to Lead,* which challenged the conventional view of American power in decline. America is still a very powerful country. How do you see the development of American soft power since then and what can we learn from this experience? For example, America still has the best universities that attract talent from all over the world. How has the impact of the Trump administration in the last several years affected American soft power?

Joseph S. Nye Jr.: Well, soft power is the ability to influence others through attraction rather than coercion or payment. I first developed this idea back in 1989 and 1990, when there was a widespread belief at the time that America was in decline, and I thought that was incorrect. But after I totaled up the usual resources of military power and economic power and so forth, I [felt] there was still something missing, which is the ability to attract, and that's why I developed this concept of soft power.

Now, if you look back over the years, American soft power goes up and down over time. In the last four years under President Trump, we've seen a considerable loss of American soft power. Trump's populist nationalism and his attitudes in general made America less attractive. I think that the last four years have been bad years for American soft power. You can measure that by looking at public opinion polls like Pew polls or Gallup polls and so forth of international opinion. On the other hand, I think it's likely that American soft power will recover under President Biden. He's already reversed some of the things that Trump did which were particularly unpopular, such as the withdrawal from the Paris Climate Accords or withdrawal from the World Health Organization. So those are things that help. In addition, [Biden's] attitudes more generally, I think, are less nativist, nationalist, and therefore will make the US more attractive to other countries.

Does this indicate American decline? The interesting thing to me is that there are always beliefs that America is in decline. It comes in cycles. And what [these views] miss is the ability of the Americans to be resilient, to regenerate themselves. Take the 1960s, the US was extremely unpopular around the world because of the Vietnam War. But by the 1970s and 80s, American soft power had been restored. So, in that sense, though we've had a bad four years under Trump, I don't regard that as a sign of American decline. I think it's more typical of the cycles that we've gone through in the past, and I expect that [the US] will probably recover from this one, as we have from others in the past.

Huiyao Wang: The world has changed a lot since the end of the twentieth century. During the first 20 years of this century, we have seen globalization expanding rapidly and multinational corporations (MNCs) operating more widely around the world. But there is an idea that while MNCs have expanded their operations, they have not brought sufficient benefits to their home or host countries. For example, in the US, the gap between rich and poor has widened, contributing to the rise of populism and nationalism. What do you think about this kind of "deglobalization" that damages soft power, not only for the US but for other countries as well? Have we seen setbacks for soft power?

Joseph S. Nye Jr.: Well, I think you're right that one of the things that globalization has done is to produce challenges to different groups within domestic society, which has stimulated populist and nationalistic reactions. If you're a factory worker in, let's say, the middle of the US, and you lose your job because the job is going to China or to Vietnam, you're not likely to be in favor of globalization and you'll react against this, and many such people wound up being voters for President Trump. Then again, I think you could argue that this increased inequalities; while some people benefited from globalization, others didn't, and that rising inequality is another tension in the political system. So, a country's soft power depends not just on the words that it says, but on the deeds that it does and the way that it practices its own values at home. In that sense, we've seen that globalization has produced a degree of populist reaction, which has produced a polarization in politics, which has undercut the attractiveness or soft power of the US. I think that is a real factor. One of the things that President Biden is doing is focusing on his domestic agenda to try to cure many of those aspects, and I think that he is headed in the right direction for that.

But it's true that globalization produces a reaction, and that reaction can undercut soft power. This doesn't mean that soft power is less important, but it does mean that it's hard to maintain under conditions like that. What you see when you have disruptive social change is a tendency to populism and nationalism. And you see this in many countries. Nationalism [may become] attractive to people inside the country, but almost by definition, since [nationalism] sets a country apart in an antagonistic role, it's not attractive to others. This is a problem for the US and for China, too. If you take the so-called "wolf warrior" diplomacy, that might be popular inside China as part of a response to Chinese nationalism, but it's not very popular in other countries.

Huiyao Wang: You raised a good comment in an article you wrote for *The Wall Street Journal* in 2005 on the rise of Chinese soft power, which referred to [NBA star] Yao Ming, the film *Crouching Tiger, Hidden Dragon*, and the Beijing Olympics.

China has a 5000-year history and rich cultural resources such as Confucianism. We see that Chinese collectivism can have advantages when it comes to helping China fight climate change or the pandemic. So, how do you see Chinese soft power and what could be done to enhance it?

Joseph S. Nye Jr.: Chinese soft power has many sources. One, of course, is Chinese traditional culture, which is very attractive. Indeed, the very idea of soft power can be traced back to great Chinese thinkers like Lao-Tzu. I may have coined the words "soft power," but the concept of influencing others by attraction is an ancient Chinese philosophy. So, Chinese traditional culture is a source of soft power for China. Another major source of soft power is China's remarkable economic performance. China has raised hundreds of millions of people out of poverty in the last 40 years. This is widely admired and provides attraction and influence for China.

If there are deep sources for China's soft power, I think there are also problems. One is that when you have conflict with your neighbors—for example, China has conflicts with many countries related to the South China Sea or its borders with India—that makes it hard to generate soft power in those countries. You can set up a Confucius Institute in New Delhi and teach Chinese culture, but you're not going to attract Indians if Chinese soldiers are killing Indian soldiers on the Himalayan border.

So, one problem for Chinese soft power is the existence of these territorial conflicts with a number of its neighbors. Another limit on China's soft power is the insistence on tight Party control of civil society. A great deal of a country's soft power is produced not by its government, but by its civil society. [Civil society] makes a country more attractive and more resilient. If the Party insists on clamping down on everything in civil society, that makes it less flexible, less attractive. If you have a creative genius produced by Chinese civil society, the best thing to do is to celebrate that, not to try and control it. We saw this just this week. Chloe Zhao, the Chinese film director who won the Oscar for the best director; that should be celebrated in China, not censored.

Huiyao Wang: I think there are different interpretations of that. China has 1.4 billion people and developing the standards and measures of soft power will be a gradual process. For example, with a 5000-year history of collective society, people are willing to sacrifice some individual freedoms for the sake of the community. This has worked well in fighting COVID-19 in China. In China, basically, you can now go anywhere and there are no more COVID-19 cases. So, I think some of those things are a changing dynamic. But there's always room to improve.

In your recent book, *Do Morals Matter?* you analyze the role of ethics in US foreign policy in the American era after 1945 from FDR to President Trump. As we are now facing a more complex world, what do you think about President Biden as he reaches 100 days in office, having analyzed the previous 14 presidents before him?

Joseph S. Nye Jr. : [For] Biden, it's still much soon to judge him historically, because we have only seen three months of his presidency. But [so far] he seems to be doing pretty well. President Trump took a position of being divisive for political support. His popularity with the US public never rose above 50 percent. Present Biden has taken a different approach, which is trying to appeal more broadly. His popularity is somewhere around 57 percent. That's an indication of a different style of leadership and is a good sign for the future, but it's much too early to judge at this stage.

Huiyao Wang: Do you think that President Biden and President Xi, with the world facing the pandemic and climate change, can demonstrate some kind of moral relationship? If China and the US can work together to fight the pandemic, we'd probably have a much more organized world. I think that kind of moral leadership is important for both President Biden and President Xi.

Joseph S. Nye Jr.: Exactly right, I'm sure. I've argued that we have to think of the US–China relationship as what I call a "cooperative rivalry." There will be areas of rivalry. For example, different views on the navigation of the South China Sea will be an area of traditional rivalry. But [things are different] when it comes to ecological interdependence, which is illustrated by climate or by pandemics. Viruses do not respect nationality, they just want to reproduce themselves, so they cross borders without any respect to what governments say or to politics. The same thing is true with greenhouse gases. In that sense, we have to be able to realize that ecological interdependence, which is a form of globalization, is [something] that requires cooperation. So, while there will be rivalry in certain areas, there has to be cooperation at the same time. At this virtual climate summit held by President Biden last week, I was pleased to see President Xi, President Putin, and others, because it really is essential that we overcome rivalries in areas where we must cooperate. There's no alternative to cooperation.

Huiyao Wang: You've previously said that the development of soft power need not be a zero-sum game. Do you think that both the US and China could gain soft power from cooperating in certain areas? For example, President Biden has announced a major infrastructure plan and

China has become a leader in infrastructure over the past four decades, being home to two-thirds of the total length of high-speed rail and seven of the ten largest container ports. Maybe China and the US could work together on infrastructure or on the global fight against COVID-19—could this help to increase the soft power of both sides and encourage more cooperation?

Joseph S. Nye Jr.: I think that's correct. Soft power doesn't have to be zero-sum. If, for example, China becomes more attractive in the US, and the US becomes more attractive in China—that can help both of us overcome our differences.

Some years ago, I co-authored an article with a distinguished Chinese scholar, Wang Jisi of Peking University. We pointed out in that article that soft power can be positive-sum in which both sides can benefit simultaneously—not always, but in some instances. And that's why it's important for the US and China to find areas where they can cooperate because we both look more attractive in the eyes of other countries if we do so. Most countries don't want to have to choose in a harsh way between China and the US. To that extent, when we are cooperating, particularly on the production of global public goods, as you can imagine, that increases China's soft power and increases American soft power at the same time. At the Boao Forum [for Asia in April 2021] I mentioned the idea that the US and China could work together on the idea of strengthening health systems for poor countries, including their vaccine capabilities, which would be good for us as well as good for them, and which would also enhance the soft power of both our countries.

Huiyao Wang: China and the US are the two largest economies in the world and the US has been a leader in building the post-war system of global governance. China has benefited greatly from this system and is now more active in trying to add to it. So, there is great potential to work together.

I notice that you've questioned the model of the Thucydides Trap in which a rising power challenges the ruling power; that part of this could be a genuine challenge, and that fear also plays a role, and that this situation can cause a self-fulfilling prophecy of conflict, but that we should not overemphasize this aspect. That's an interesting view that maybe you can elaborate on. Because we don't want to get into any deadly confrontation, we are so interdependent now.

Joseph S. Nye Jr.: I think that's right. A rising power can create fear in an established power and that can be the source of conflict, but it doesn't have to be. Even thinking back to the Peloponnesian War, which Thucydides described, he said the causes of the war were the rise and the power of Athens and the fear it created in Sparta. We can control the amount of fear—if we become too obsessive about fear of each other, then we could fall into something like the Thucydides trap.

My own view is that we don't have to succumb to that fear. Basically, as I see it, China does not pose an existential threat to the US and the US doesn't pose an existential threat to China. We're not trying to take over China. So, in that sense, we will compete, but we should limit the fears. It's not as though it's life-or-death fears. In that sense, going back to Thucydides: the rise in China's power will likely continue, there's not much we can do about that. Only China will do something about it, which is how it behaves domestically. But the fear that this creates in the US is something we *can* do something about, which is to not exaggerate [the threat from] China, to not become overly fearful. Competition is healthy. Frankly, the idea that the Americans will improve some things at home, such as infrastructure, because China is leading the way for example on high-speed rail, that can be healthy. But if it becomes obsessively fearful, it can become destructive.

So, my view is that we should be careful of the language we use. I don't like this language some people are using about a new "Cold War" between the US and China. I think that's a misreading of history. It implies a deeper and more intractable conflict than is really the case. If you look back to the real Cold War between the US and the Soviet Union, there was almost no economic interdependence, whereas with the US and China [today], you find just the opposite—half a trillion dollars [in bilateral] trade. If you look back on the real Cold War, there was no social interdependence, whereas today more than 3 million Chinese come to the US as tourists and 300,000 as students. So, there is much greater economic interdependence, social interdependence, and ecological interdependence. During the Cold War, we were less worried about climate change or pandemics. [Increasing] globalization and interdependence urge us to be careful about not using metaphors like the Cold War, which were [apt] for a time in history, but not necessarily accurate descriptions of the current period of history.

Huiyao Wang: Absolutely. The term "Cold War" is really obsolete when we have such deep economic interdependence, social dependence, ecological dependence, and technology interdependence. So, decoupling or confrontation between China and the US does not make sense.

I remember last time when you were in China you talked about "cooperative rivalry." What can China and the US do to achieve a healthy cooperative rivalry?

Joseph S. Nye Jr.: One thing is to strengthen the ties that we have—students, visitors, communication—these are important aspects of what I call "social interdependence" which help to develop deeper understanding between [our] societies.

The other is on economic interdependence. There will be some areas where there will be decoupling, in areas that touch on [security issues]. For example, Americans are very worried about Huawei or ZTE controlling 5G telecommunications in the US for security reasons. I don't think you can see more economic interdependence [in this area], just as China doesn't want to allow Google or Facebook to operate freely inside China because of security reasons. So, there will be some areas where there will be decoupling. But that doesn't mean we want to see overall economic decoupling, which would be extraordinarily costly for both countries.

Finally, we have this question of how we manage the relationship overall so that we avoid miscalculations or accidents. People who talk about 1945 in the Cold War are picking the wrong date for a historical analogy. As Henry Kissinger points out, 1914 is something we should pay more attention to. At the time, none of the great powers in Europe wanted a world war. They expected their competition in the Balkans to see a short, sharp conflict that would redress the balance of power, and then things would go back to normal. Instead, through miscalculations and failure to manage the competitive parts of the relationship, they wound up with four years of war, which destroyed four empires and destroyed the centrality of Europe in the global balance of power.

We have to be extremely cautious and careful that we don't allow some incident in the South China Sea or over Taiwan to lead us into something which nobody intends with great unintended consequences. That's going to require constant communication, so we need to enhance our cooperation in areas of interdependence where it's possible to cooperate, but in the areas which are competitive we have to be much more cautious and attentive in how we communicate with each other to [avoid] miscalculations. Those are the two things I think we have to do to avoid this relationship becoming a zero-sum game.

As I mentioned earlier, I remain relatively optimistic about the long run. But humans make mistakes. That's the nature of being human so we have to guard against those mistakes.

Huiyao Wang: Absolutely, it's important to promote mutual understanding and avoid miscalculations, as disasters can happen.

I remember that you have said that a new Cold War is not possible, for several reasons. Americans shouldn't be too worried about China; geographically, the US is far [from China] and has friendly neighbors. Also, the US is already self-sufficient in energy, while China is still dependent on imports. Technology-wise, the US remains in the lead in many areas. So, the US shouldn't have such great cause for concern about China.

I hope we can build trust in China–US relations. As we approach the end of President Biden's first 100 days in office, how can we shape a different perspective for the future of US–China relations?

Joseph S. Nye Jr.: One of the things that both of us have to worry about is the rise of nationalism in our two countries. I mentioned earlier that the effect of globalization on creating inequality and disrupting jobs and so forth led to more populist and nativist nationalism in the US and that produced voters for President Trump. But let's be frank, there's also rising nationalism in China. If you look at the Chinese web, you'll notice enormous nationalism. In China, there's still this argument about overcoming nineteenth-century history as a form of recruiting support. Things like "wolf warrior" diplomacy are very popular inside China. But those things are not healthy in terms of creating trust in other countries.

Take, for example, the program, [Made in China 2025], about [developing homegrown] technologies. That made sense inside China but created fear in Washington. The fact that China was going to try to replace the US in a whole series of important technologies created fear in Washington. Or when President Xi Jinping said that China would be number one in artificial intelligence by 2030, that was read in Washington as well—that China intends to replace the US by 2030. It might have been a good goal in terms of recruiting national support inside China, but every political leader faces what's called the "two–audience problem." One audience is internal, the other audience is external, and sometimes messages that play well internally play badly externally. I think both [the US and China], given the rise in nationalism that's produced to some extent by globalization, have to be careful about the two–audience problem.

Huiyao Wang: You are correct. For the competition to remain peaceful, it is important to pay attention to domestic politics and prevent populism from getting out of hand. In America, there is a widening gap between rich and poor and major racial divides. In the last several decades, China has been trying to reduce the income inequality gap, though there remain significant urban–rural differences. China has been working to lift 800 million people out of extreme poverty so that poverty doesn't generate populism and dissatisfaction with globalization or China's opening–up. I think that lessons can be learned for both countries.

One problem is how we can get multinational corporations and other players such as non-government and non-profit organizations to work together for a more inclusive and balanced form of globalization, particularly in developing countries. Also, given the impact of COVID-19 in developing countries, it's crucial that the US and China work together. Last weekend, we celebrated the 50th anniversary of "ping pong diplomacy" between China and the US. The slogan then was, "friendship first, competition second." As a professor that has seen many ups and downs in the bilateral relationship, what's your take on the future of Sino-US relations? I have noticed you have outlined quite a few scenarios for the future.

Joseph S. Nye Jr.: One could imagine a variety of scenarios. Any time you try to guess the future, you have to realize that there is no "one" future. There are many possible futures and they're affected by [unexpected] events that we don't yet know and also affected by our own actions and [behaviors]. One can imagine futures of US–China relations which are bad or good. What we then have to [consider] is, what are the things we can do to steer toward the good relations which are beneficial to both.

When you look back historically, since 1945, we've gone through a series of [phases in the US–China] relationship. In the first 20 years or so, things were pretty tough. After all, the US and Chinese soldiers fought each other on the Korean Peninsula in the 1950s. So, we had twenty years of a tense relationship. Then, as you pointed out, we had ping pong diplomacy and the easing of relations, Nixon's visit to Beijing, and another 20 years of improving relations. During the Clinton administration, there was a desire to integrate [a rising] China into the international order through the World Trade Organization and so forth. That lasted nearly 20 years, but with the arrival of Donald Trump in 2015–2016, there was a feeling among many Americans that China was not playing fair—that it was subsidizing state-owned enterprises, stealing intellectual property, and militarizing islands in the South China Sea, which President Xi had promised President Obama he would not do. Then there was a reaction against this, so we started another cycle. So, we've gone through ups and downs roughly every twenty years. [Taking] that same 20-year cycle, we're [now] in the middle—it started around 2015 and through 2025 will be 10 years. I hope it doesn't have to last that long, but it's quite possible that we'll have intense competition for 20 years.

My own personal view is that China [isn't] a threat to the existence of the US, [nor is] the US a threat to the existence of China. So, in that sense, I think that you could imagine some period—who knows, maybe 2035—when you'll see the cycle turn toward better relations, or maybe even sooner than that. But again, as with any time you predict the future, you have to realize that history is always full of surprises. Every time you think you know something, there's going to be something which you haven't taken into account. So that makes it more important that we try to [act] cautiously so that we don't get the wrong sorts of surprises.

Huiyao Wang: I agree with you, China is not a threat to the US and hopefully the US is not a threat to China.

In one of your Project Syndicate articles [published in October 2020], you talked about five scenarios for the international order in 2030. Scenario one was that the liberal international order could come to an end because of populism and other political forces. The second scenario was something similar to the 1930s, with massive unemployment, economic depression, and politicians taking advantage of this situation to promote populist protectionism. Scenario three was China being more active in the international arena or dominating the global order, with China's GDP surpassing that of the US. The fourth scenario discussed the global green agenda, such as climate change and a "COVID Marshall Plan." The fifth scenario emphasized similarities and coexistence between countries. We've talked about China and the US, so let's [take a look] into your crystal ball for the future of the entire world.

Joseph S. Nye Jr.: I do think that you're going to see an increased importance of the green agenda, simply because this is something which obeys the laws of physics and biology, not politics. As more and more people and countries become aware of the importance of climate change and the dangers of things like pandemics, I think that's going to put pressure on political leaders to take these issues more seriously than they have in the past. It's not going to totally replace traditional politics and traditional competition by any means, but it will become increasingly important. That means that the cooperative dimensions [of the international order] are going to have to increase.

Political leaders could still make mistakes and fail to see this or react to it. But I do think that it's a source of potential optimism, that this agenda [will become increasingly important] because of physics and biology. So, of the various scenarios that I sketched out for the world in that Project Syndicate column, I saw the gradual evolution of the world as we see it now as the most likely. But I put more emphasis on the green agenda now than I would have before COVID, so I remain relatively optimistic that we can pull through this period.

Huiyao Wang: I'm glad you're cautiously optimistic because all countries are so dependent on each other.

We now have over 800,000 people tuned in to our dialogue [...] So, as a final conclusion, what would you like to say to this large audience today?

Joseph S. Nye Jr.: Well, we're all human. We're bound to make mistakes. There are bound to be tensions and competition between Chinese and Americans. But we have to keep it in perspective. We have more in common and more to gain from cooperation, and we have to keep that perspective. So, I think if we have an optimistic view about our potential to manage competition and to practice cooperation, I think we can look to a good future.

Huiyao Wang: Great, Professor Nye, thank you so much, we appreciate you taking the time to talk with me. We hope to see you next time. We also want to thank our audience in China and the rest of the world.

Thucydides's Trap Revisited: Prospects for China–US Relations

A Dialogue with Graham Allison and Chen Li

Huiyao Wang, Graham Allison, and Chen Li

On April 6, 2021, CCG hosted a dialogue between CCG President Huiyao Wang, Graham Allison, Douglas Dillon Professor of Government at Harvard University, and Chen Li, Director of the Center for International Security and Strategy at the School of International Studies, Renmin University of China.

Graham Allison is a world-renowned political scientist and an influential voice in US thinking on strategy and national security. He has special interests in nuclear weapons, Russia, China, and decision-making. Allison has taught at Harvard University for five decades, where he was the founding dean of the Harvard Kennedy School and former director of the Belfer Center for Science and International Affairs. He has also served

H. Wang (✉)
Center for China and Globalization (CCG), Beijing, China

G. Allison
Harvard Kennedy School, Cambridge, MA, USA

C. Li
Renmin University of China, Beijing, China

H. Wang and L. Miao (eds.), *Understanding Globalization, Global Gaps, and Power Shifts in the 21st Century*,
https://doi.org/10.1007/978-981-19-3846-7_9

in a number of senior roles in the US government, including Special Advisor to the Secretary of Defense under President Reagan and Assistant Secretary of Defense under President Clinton.

Allison is the author of many best-selling books, including *Essence of Decision: Explaining the Cuban Missile Crisis* (1971), *Nuclear Terrorism: The Ultimate Preventable Catastrophe* (2004), *Lee Kuan Yew: The Grand Master's Insights on China, the United States and the World* (2013). His 2017 book *Destined for War: Can America and China Escape Thucydides's Trap?* is one of the most cited works on China–US relations in recent times and has established an influential framework for thinking about great power relations, as explored in this dialogue.

For this conversation, we were also lucky to be joined by Chen Li from the School of International Studies at Renmin University. Li's extensive research on modern military and strategic history, international history, and China–US relations made him ideally placed to bring a Chinese historical perspective to this discussion.

This talk took place toward the end of President Biden's first 100 days in office. After the tumultuous tenure of President Trump, many observers were looking for a change of course in foreign policy under Biden, including a return to multilateralism and recalibration of Washington's stance toward China. In our discussion, we looked ahead to prospects for China–US relations under the new president. We also revisited the idea of Thucydides's Trap—a deadly pattern of structural stress that results when a rising power challenges a ruling one—as well as other historical examples such as the Cold War, the Concert of Europe, and the Chanyuan Treaty of 1005, to draw out lessons that might help to prevent conflict in our current age.

Huiyao Wang: The question posed by the title of your book *Destined for War? Can America and China Escape Thucydides's Trap?* has become a famous one. Greek historian Thucydides wrote that the rise of Athens and the fear that this instilled in Sparta made war inevitable. Can America and China escape this trap? It's been four years since you published the book, so maybe you can share some of your new thinking on this topic. You have compared China and the US to inseparable conjoined twins in which if one gives way to its impulses in dealing with the other and strangles it, it will succeed in killing its twin, but it will commit suicide.

Graham Allison: Thank you very much. I've long argued that the Chinese should be much more forthcoming in helping all of us appreciate more of what Xi Jinping now calls "Chinese wisdom." Actually, I applauded the fact that he's been more forward-leaning about the idea that maybe China has learned something that the rest of us could learn from. I'm eager to hear what others have to say on the topic but I have a pretty good idea of what I think. Let me make three points just to start with.

First point, for those who may not remember Thucydides's Trap and the Thucydides rivalry. The point which I make in my book, and which I would urge you to think about if you haven't had a chance to look at it, is that the defining feature of the relationship between the US and China today, for as far ahead as I can see, will be a ruthless rivalry. So, a competition in which a rising China—which is seeking to "make China great again" and will continue as it has for a generation, rising, and becoming stronger—and as it does, it will be encroaching on positions and prerogatives that Americans, as the ruling power, have come to believe are naturally their own as number one, at the top of every pecking order.

If we put this against the canvas of history, the best way to clarify what's actually happening in this relationship is that China is rising. As long as China doesn't crash or crack up, it will continue rising. So currently, it has about one-quarter of the per capita GDP of the US, but of course, it also has four times as many people. On the current trajectory, why shouldn't the Chinese be as productive as the South Koreans? Of course, they will be. If they [do become this productive], China will have more than half of the per capita GDP of the US and a GDP twice the size of the US. So, as China rises in every arena, Americans, who have become accustomed to believing we are number one in every competition, will find themselves being overtaken.

At the beginning of the century, America was the major trading partner of everybody. By 2021, China is the major trading partner of almost everybody. A generation ago, America was the manufacturing workshop of the world. Today, China is the manufacturer of the world. So, in terms of structural realities, a rising China is impacting a ruling US. In my book, I compare this to a seesaw of power in which China inevitably gets stronger, wealthier, and more powerful. That's the nature of the Thucydides' rivalry. That rise shifts the tectonics of power, the seesaw of power between the rising power and the ruling power. That's point one. I know many Chinese colleagues have not wanted to accept this proposition, saying that China is not really rising, but that it's already risen or that China is different. I would say the best way to think about it is that this is another instance of a pattern that we've seen since Thucydides wrote about Athens and Sparta. In my book, I find 16 instances of [such a situation] just in the last 500 years, so this has been occurring for a long time.

Point two is equally important. The objective conditions of the twenty-first century have condemned the US and China to co-exist since the only other option is to co-destruct. There are two arenas here. First, nuclear weapons. In the Cold War, we learned very painfully when the Soviet Union acquired a robust nuclear arsenal that was capable of a second strike, that we lived in a "MAD" world of Mutually Assured Destruction. That means that if one [power] attacked the other, at the end of the story, both would be destroyed. So, this is like a mutual suicide pact. I have compared it to inseparable conjoined twins in which, if one gives way to its impulses in dealing with the other and strangles it, it will succeed in killing its twin, but it will also commit suicide. So that's the nuclear arena, and it's true in the US–China relationship today. Even though the US has a much larger nuclear arsenal, it's still the case that if there was a full-scale nuclear war, at the end of the war, America would be destroyed. So that's mutually assured destruction. In the twenty-first century, we also have the climate issue. China, the number one greenhouse gas emitter, and the US, which is the number two emitter, inhabit the same contained biosphere. Either nation can, by themselves, create an environment in which neither can live. So, we have a kind of a "climate MAD" analog to the nuclear situation.

In addition, [the US and China] are both so entangled in the process of globalization and the global economy that neither can "decouple" itself from the other without impoverishing itself. So, on the one hand, [the US and China] are going to be fierce rivals. On the other hand, we're condemned by nature and by technology to cooperate in order to survive. So, what if these two contradictory ideas hold at the same time? That's why in searching for ways to escape Thucydides's Trap, I found [the following] bit of Chinese wisdom very interesting.

As best I can understand it, in the Song Dynasty, back a thousand years ago, in 1005, the Song, having found themselves unable to defeat the Liao, a northern Mongol tribe, negotiated the Chanyuan Treaty, in which as some historians have called it, they agreed to become "rivalry partners." They defined areas in which they would continue to be rivals, but they had other areas in which they were thickly cooperating. In fact, it was a very peculiar arrangement, because even though the Liao agreed that the Song was the major dynasty, the tribute actually flowed from the Song to the Liao; the Song was paying the Liao. The deal was that the Liao had to take whatever tribute was paid and use it to buy things from the Song. [This created] an early version of the multiplier effect in economics. I know some Chinese don't like this treaty because, for whatever reason, the Song dynasty is not appreciated sufficiently. That's my poor man's view of Chinese history, so apologies for that. But in any case, from my perspective, since I'm interested in avoiding war, it is the Chanyuan Treaty that preserved peace between the Song and the Liao for 120 years. I would say in the annals of history, a treaty that takes two parties who are in fierce rivalry and manages [to deliver] 100 years of peace between them has done a pretty good thing.

Huiyao Wang: Thank you for this great illustration of your points. I really like your twin metaphor. We are now in a deeply entwined world where countries such as China and the US are inseparable like conjoined twins. We have to work together to fight climate change, the pandemic, and address all our other shared challenges. If [China and the US] really separate, we will both die in the end.

In *Destined for War?* you describe 16 cases in which a rising power has confronted a ruling power in the last 500 years. Of these cases, four of them ended peacefully. Professor Li is a military strategy researcher and as Graham has mentioned, in the context of the Song-Liao relationship in Chinese history, the Chanyuan Treaty actually secured peace for almost 100–200 years, during which time there were 380 representative exchanges. So, there is a precedent for rival powers being able to maintain peace. Professor Li, perhaps you can share some of your ideas on how we can avoid Thucydides's Trap, based on your research.

Chen Li: Thank you Huiyao and thank you, Graham. I have a few comments on Graham's remarks. Firstly, I think with regard to both the concept of the rising and ruling powers, in particular, for the experience of both the rise of the US in the nineteenth century or early twentieth century and the rise of China in the last 70 years, the most important factor is the home front. That is, we need to concentrate on our economic development at home and on solving our own social problems. I think this is one of the most important lessons.

My second point is that with regard to the challenges and risks of great power competition, I totally agree with Graham. During the Cold War, nuclear weapons were extremely dangerous. In the twenty-first century, we also have other new technological challenges, such as cyber issues, which play a huge role in our daily life. If great power competition escalates, I think we will face serious challenges in the cyber domain, so we need to manage this competition very carefully.

My third point is about the relationship between the Liao and the Song, as mentioned by Graham. I have two points here. The first is that we probably need to adopt a long-term perspective because the Song-Liao experience was a long peace after a long war. Both sides learned plenty of lessons from the long war which lasted over 30 years. One challenge in the twenty-first century is that we can't have a long period of peace after a long war, because war is too destructive in the current age.

My fourth point is that the reason why the Song and the Liao were able to achieve a long peace is that they realized that you can't rely on force to solve all of your problems. You always have other concerns such as external challenges and also you need to focus on your home front, as just mentioned.

Graham Allison: Can I ask Chen Li one question, please? Looking at the Song and their relationship with the Liao, is this a special case in Chinese history or are there some analogs that you would regard as similar from which we might also learn something?

Chen Li: In ancient China, the major dynasties—not only the Song, but also the Han and other dynasties—tried to improve their policies to maintain peace with all other entities. We can probably find other periods of peace. I think that this is a very interesting area for our research. That's something we can learn from you because you pay more attention to the lessons from ancient history for contemporary history or current affairs. We need more cooperation between historians who work on ancient Chinese history and experts who work on current affairs.

Graham Allison: In the US and England, where you studied, there are many people who study Chinese dynasties. It's fascinating because it's such a long history. It's so complex and for a poor person like me, who doesn't speak Mandarin and comes late to the party, it's staggering. As for the US, I have trouble thinking of 300 years of history. So, for 3000 years or more with so many twists and turns, it's a very rich body of experience that ought to be processed for lessons and I think Chinese historians, obviously, have an advantage in that. But there are many people in the

West interested, so I hope you and your colleagues dig in further. It was only by accident that I was introduced to this case, as somebody once told me about the Song and Liao as an example. But I bet there are more examples I just haven't found yet.

Huiyao Wang: In Chinese history, there are probably many cases where conflict was avoided and peace was secured. For example, in the Ming Dynasty, Zheng He led seven expeditions to go as far as Africa and Southeast Asia, 100 years before Columbus reached America. During these trips, Zheng He's expedition gave many gifts to other countries and locals and never colonized any other nations. Historically, China has been relatively peace-loving. As of now, the PRC still hasn't sent a soldier to occupy any foreign territory.

Graham, your recent article in *Foreign Affairs* called for the Biden administration to adopt an "unsentimental China policy." Do you view the essence of the US–China rivalry as based on structural change or something more complicated—a combination of fear, values, psychology, ideological differences, or even a clash of civilizations? And what can we do about this?

Graham Allison: I think the good news about Biden is that he is somebody who is well-grounded and has thought about international affairs for all of his adult life. I've known him now for more than four decades. He has been in the Senate, he's been the chairman of the Foreign Relations Committee, and he has been the vice president. He and Xi Jinping have probably spent more time together than any other leaders, other than Putin, or before that, Lee Kuan Yew. They understand each other. So, when they had this phone call [in February 2021], they were not starting from scratch. They're building on a relationship that's already developed.

I think President Biden appreciates the fact, as I've written, that the challenge is the "Fitzgerald Challenge." In his 1936 essay, "The Crack-Up," Scott Fitzgerald writes that the test of a first-class mind is the ability to hold two contradictory ideas in your head at the same time and still function. Idea one is that this is going to be a fierce competition, because both the US and China are determined, to whatever extent they can, to be the biggest economy, the smartest economy, have the best AI, the best military, and be the biggest trading partner, and so on. When the Olympics occur, each nation will be seeking to win as much gold as they can. That's what the Olympics are. That's on the one hand.

On the other hand, at the same time, and somewhat in contradiction with the first idea, is the fact that unless the US and China can find ways to coordinate and cooperate in dealing with climate, we will create a biosphere that nobody can live in. Unless the US and China can find a way to cooperate to make sure third-party actions, like events over Taiwan or North Korea, don't spiral out of control, or we could end up in a real full-scale war. We could end up destroying both societies. Most people can't imagine what that means today, but during the Cold War, we used to look at target charts and calculate the destructive effects. It could literally be the case that if we had a full-scale nuclear war between China and the US, both China and the US would be wiped off the map, they'd simply be gone as countries. But that's inconceivable. No human being can make sense of that, but that's the physical capability of the weapons that exist. So, we are compelled to cooperate, to avoid sequences of events that could lead to that result, and to avoid letting unconstrained greenhouse gas emissions create a globe that we can't live or breathe in.

So, how to do these two things at the same time? And how to explain this in the complicated politics of both countries? Because Americans look at China and say, "My God! How could China be rivaling us on all these fronts? We remember when China was small, poor, and backward as a developing country." And Chinese, when they watch what happened in Anchorage [the US–China meeting in March 2021] or other events, and when I read of people who watch Chinese social media, some people say, "Enough of this, we don't need to have an American lecturing us anymore. We have become bigger and stronger, we need to be more assertive." So, on managing the internal affairs of two great powers, I think Xi Jinping and Biden may be able to hold two contradictory ideas and function, but how can they manage their governments and their societies under these conditions? That's the problem I have been working on. But I don't have too many good ideas.

Huiyao Wang: I like your idea of the Olympic Games spirit. If we can conduct a peaceful competition where we all strive for gold medals, maybe we can achieve a win–win situation. Maybe we should measure countries by key performance indicators (KPIs) related to domestic performance. It's like Deng Xiaoping's idea that "it doesn't matter if the cat is black or white, as long as it catches mice." Rather than picking out each other's problems, we should concentrate on solving our own problems. So, I think this idea of the Olympic Games spirit is really suitable in the context of Sino–US relations.

Next, I'd like to discuss the 12 clues for peace you mention in *Destined for War: Can America and China Escape Thucydides's Trap?* The first is that higher authorities can help resolve rivalry without war, such as international organizations. Second, states can be embedded in larger economic, political, and security institutions that constrain historically "normal" behaviors. This point is also very relevant for the contemporary world, where all countries are part of larger economic, political, and security institutions which constrain behavior.

The third clue is that wily statesmen make a virtue of necessity and distinguish needs and wants. The fourth clue is that timing is crucial. This is very true; this is a critical time as the whole world comes out of the pandemic. Fifth, cultural commonalities can help prevent conflict. We already have globalization and a relatively globalized culture. Could a deepening of this help to prevent conflict? Your sixth clue is that there's nothing new under the sun—except nuclear weapons. Seventh, mutually assured destruction is a strong deterrent against conflict. Clue eight is that a hot war between nuclear superpowers is thus no longer a justifiable option. This is also true. China and the US both have nuclear weapons, so if conflict were to be triggered and get out of control, the whole world could be destroyed.

Clue number nine is that leaders of nuclear superpowers must nonetheless be prepared to risk a war that cannot be won. This is followed by clue ten, which states that "thickening economic entanglement" between China and the US is the way to go, as economic interdependence raises the cost of war, and thus lowers the likelihood it will occur. Clue 11 is that alliances can be a fatal attraction and clue 12 is that domestic performance is decisive. This is also correct—we should all focus on domestic performance, which is to measure a nation by how it is able to support its people. For example, China has lifted 800 million people out of poverty, which is perhaps the most significant human rights development in China in recent times. So, all 12 clues laid out in your book still largely hold true. I don't know if you or Professor Li have anything to add on this?

Chen Li: I would say a few things. As Graham mentioned in his earlier comments, he is convinced that the leaders of China and the US are determined to manage their competition, but he's not so sure whether society and public opinion on both sides will do so as well. Well, a positive lesson from the Cold War is that we have two periods. The first period was the mobilization of both sides. At that time, people probably believed that force and pressure would work. But I think later on, both sides realized that pressure and force had limitations. So, the mobilization period of great power competition passed and the world entered into détente, a period of stabilization.

The key point here is that if we can manage crisis very carefully and we review the lessons of competition—not only leaders but also ordinary citizens—then the public will realize that in the long term, we need to talk with each other and also cooperate with each other, not only to maintain peace but also to solve problems.

Graham also mentioned the important factor of other parties. Even during long-term great power competition, we need to work with both sides and with other parties to try to establish some security order to accommodate the crucial interests of everyone. I think this is why in the 1970s and in the 1980s, the Cold War in Europe was relatively quiet compared to the 1940s and 1950s, when we witnessed plenty of crises.

Graham Allison: I agree very much. The Cold War started with the idea that these are two systems inherently so incompatible, that one will have to destroy the other, and that would normally lead to war. But initially, because the US and the Soviet Union were both exhausted from World War II, and eventually, because both sides acquired nuclear arsenals, [both sides] concluded that war was not an option. So, how about having a "war" but don't use bombs and bullets with uniformed combatants. And in that so-called Cold War, early on, there emerged a set of constraints, some of which were implicit, some of which were explicit. And then, eventually, we discovered that we would have to coordinate and constrain, but also communicate very quickly and even cooperate in order to prevent things from getting out of control. I think the lessons from that set of experiences, even though the current rivalry between US and China is very different, nonetheless can be very instructive.

For example, I was doing something on this with people in Washington last week. I was explaining that even in the deadliest era or days of the Cold War, we were keen to have thick conversations and communication between our leaders. Reagan was often criticized by his conservative Republican colleagues for wanting to spend so much time talking to his Soviet counterparts. He said it's very important to talk to them because a nuclear war cannot be won, and therefore must never be fought. He was keen to negotiate with his Soviet counterpart, even to reach arms control agreements in which the US would forego doing something Americans wanted to do, as the price for getting the Soviet Union to forego the thing that we did not want them to do.

In every one of those cases, there was a problem of trust, so you would only agree on things that you could independently verify. But this process over time stabilized to a degree and made it possible to avoid lots of potential crises that could have gone out of control—which some almost did, in the case of the Berlin Crisis or the Cuban Missile Crisis. But I think there is no reason why, in the rivalry between the US and China, we shouldn't pick up, dust off and adapt all of the lessons that we learned from that earlier period about the necessity for communication at many levels, for thick communication, for crisis management procedures, even for crisis prevention procedures. I think that would be actually a big addition that Henry and Chen Li and lots of others, might add to the list for avoiding being sucked into the vortex of the Thucydides dynamic that could ultimately drag us into a war.

Huiyao Wang: Thank you both for adding some new thinking. These are some good ideas for crisis management. You mentioned that during the Cold War, the US and the Soviet Union engaged in fierce competition but still maintained high-level dialogue. There was even the famous "kitchen debate" between Khrushchev and Nixon.

I have a recommendation to add to your list of things that can be done to ensure peace, and it involves the EU. The EU is a huge economic bloc but it is not really subject to the dynamic of Thucydides's Trap with the US, so they occupy a third-party position. This makes the EU well-placed to act as a kind of mediating power between China and the US. There could be some kind of trilateral dialogue between China, the EU, and the US, with Europe acting as a middleman helping to prevent conflict between the US and China.

The other idea draws on an article published in *Foreign Affairs* on March 23, 2021 by Richard Haass, head of the Council on Foreign Relations, saying that the global system of multilateralism is at a crossroads and the world is moving past the two-century phase of Western domination. Haass writes that Western domination will diminish not only in the material sense but also ideologically. Haass refers to the Concert of Europe, a general consensus among the Great Powers of nineteenth-century Europe to maintain the European balance of power and the integrity of territorial boundaries. Haass writes that the world needs a great power coordination mechanism and proposes a six-member group made up of the US, China, the EU, Japan, India, and Russia—an international coordination mechanism that goes beyond ideology and values.

I also saw Henry Kissinger speak at a recent Chatham House event and also at the China Development Forum about how the final issue between China and the US and other Western countries is whether they can reach an understanding with China. If not, it's almost like we are at the eve of the First World War, and if things get out of control it could be dangerous.

I'd like to hear your thoughts on these views of Richard Haass and Henry Kissinger. How can we find commonalities to work together and accept China? I find that although China is doing well on many fronts, it's still not accepted by some Western countries. China is doing well on infrastructure, on poverty alleviation, and contributes over one-third to global GDP growth. But these things are not appreciated by the public in many Western countries. How can we reconcile this gap?

Graham Allison: I agree. You have obviously been thinking about it. So, this is good and I like your list. The US could learn a lot from China in infrastructure development. In the period the US was building one high-speed rail line going from Los Angeles to Sacramento, and actually got $85 billion into it before the project was given up, China built 12,000 miles of high-speed rail.

The EU and the idea of a three-party coordination mechanism is very interesting and I have to think more about that. On the "new concert" that Richard was arguing about, I think, basically, a lot of people have taken this analog to what happened at the Congress of Vienna and the Concert of Europe. But I think the differences between circumstances today and then are so much more substantial than the similarities that it's not a very helpful analogy.

Regarding Henry [Kissinger], he believes that if we're not able to develop some implicit and explicit constraints on competition, particularly in the areas where cooperation is necessary for survival, then the outcome will be catastrophic. I agree with that. I think the place to start is that the Thucydides's rivalry, most often, leads to catastrophic destruction. That's insane—it would be insane for China and insane for the US. So, the imperative for all of us is to find a way to escape the Thucydides Trap. And that's why we're looking everywhere we can, from rivalry partnerships in the Song dynasty, or lessons from the Cold War, to lessons from the period, as Chen Li said, when the US rose to rival Britain. Wherever we can find lessons, I think we should be actively pursuing them and collecting them.

I think, fortunately, we have Xi Jinping who gets this completely, who says the reason why we need a new form of great power relations is that we know what happens in the old form, the Thucydides dynamic. Biden understands this very well. What are we worried about? He's worried that an unconstrained rivalry ends up with a catastrophic outcome. So, I think we have an open door for ideas. So that's why I applaud you for trying to stir the pot.

Chen Li: To avoid Thucydides's Trap, we must pay more attention to the consequences of the trap. This was an advantage for people who lived through the early Cold War because that generation of people were familiar with the experiences of the Second World War. And older generations were even familiar with the First World War. So, they knew what the consequences of the trap are. Later on, these people also developed their ideas about the consequences of nuclear war.

One challenge for young people today is that we have lived in peace for so long. People are excited about the progress of our countries but probably pay less attention to the consequences of great power competition and conflict. In terms of perceptions, we need to put more emphasis on the consequences of Thucydides's Trap in order to avoid it.

With regard to economic development, Graham was very generous, saying that the US needs to learn more from China. But the US also has plenty of things in its history for us to learn from as well. For example, in the early twentieth century and during the Second World War, US production was very impressive. I think there are a few lessons here. One is to concentrate on professionalism in business. The second is to improve working relations between society, government, and the business community. China learned a lot from the US business community and the efficiency of the US government in the latter part of the twentieth century. We should become more open-minded about learning lessons from others.

Huiyao Wang: Thank you, we certainly have things to learn from each other. Your advice and the concepts you have developed are valuable to all of us. We need to continue talking about how to avoid the Thucydides Trap as we navigate this "rivalry partnership" of competition but also cooperation.

Graham Allison: I think the point that Chen Li made is extremely important. Most people today have no idea what war means. Go back to World War II, during which 50 million people were killed, which is just unimaginable. What would a nuclear war mean today? A nuclear war could literally mean that Beijing is gone, disappeared. Boston, gone, disappeared. It's hard to imagine, but the physical consequence of a full-scale war between the US and China could kill every last Chinese and every last American. Anybody who survived would later say, these people were out of their minds. How did they ever let this happen? How come they didn't appreciate what a danger this was? And if they had thought about it, and then they said, well, but something happened in Taiwan, and China did this, or the US did that, and one thing led to the other and at the end, there was a war. They would ask, but did that make any sense?

It makes no sense, in the same way how people look at Europe at the end of 1918, when World War I was over; Europe, which had been the centerpiece of civilization for 500 years, had destroyed itself. Europe never became a major player in the world again in the way that it had been for the previous 500 years. Why? Because some Archduke was assassinated by a terrorist, and then "one thing led to the other" and within five weeks, all the nations of Europe were consumed by a war that made no sense. So, the painful fact that Chen Li reminds us of [is that] today nobody has really internalized how horrible a real full-scale war could be and how insane it would be.

Fortunately, there's nobody in the Pentagon who believes that war with China is a good idea, not one single person. I believe there isn't a single person in the PLA who believes that war with the US would be a good idea. That's good. But our societies need to understand this.

Even the fact the two parties understand that war is not possible doesn't mean war can't happen. Because some spiral of reactions [can] pull you somewhere we don't want to go. So that creates a compelling reason for Americans and Chinese at all levels to be talking about dangers that could get out of control and ask, what can we do about this cooperatively with respect to North Korea? What can we do about differences over Taiwan? What can we do about patrols in the South China Sea or the East China Sea? So, I think across the whole spectrum, if we took seriously Chen Li's point about how damaging war would be, we would be much more motivated to do a lot more on that front than we are today.

Huiyao Wang: Thank you. You've really given us a good reminder today. We should really try to avoid any kind of war, especially one on a scale that could lead to the destruction of everything. I'm glad we've had a productive discussion exploring ways to escape the Thucydides Trap—the question of this century which we are all pondering.

Think Tank Dialogue: Balancing Competition and Cooperation in China–US Relations

A Dialogue with Adam S. Posen, J. Stapleton Roy, John L. Thornton, and Zhu Guangyao

Huiyao Wang, Adam S. Posen, J. Stapleton Roy,
John L. Thornton, and Zhu Guangyao

Sometimes, when bilateral tensions are high or global issues are too contentious for governments to navigate successfully alone, informal or Track II diplomacy can provide a valuable channel to maintain channels for communication and find common ground. In recent years, as frictions between China and the US have risen, CCG has increased its efforts

H. Wang (✉)
Center for China and Globalization (CCG), Beijing, China

A. S. Posen
The Peterson Institute for International Economics (PIIE),
Washington, DC, USA

J. S. Roy
Wilson Center, Washington, DC, USA

J. L. Thornton
Barrick Gold Corporation, Toronto, ON, Canada

© The Author(s) 2022   163
H. Wang and L. Miao (eds.), *Understanding Globalization,*
Global Gaps, and Power Shifts in the 21st Century,
https://doi.org/10.1007/978-981-19-3846-7_10

to build bridges and promote understanding between the two countries through Track II diplomacy. This includes outreach missions to engage counterparts in the US, hosting visiting delegations in China, and developing new platforms for exchange between think tanks, scholars, and business leaders.

On July 30, 2021, CCG continued these efforts by hosting a special dialogue between experts from Chinese and US think tanks as part of CCG's annual China and Globalization Forum. The discussion featured experts from CCG, the think tank of China's Ministry of Finance, and four leading US-based institutions: the Peterson Institute for International Economics, The Wilson Center, the Brookings Institution, and The Asia Society.

Adam S. Posen is President of the Peterson Institute for International Economics, recognized as the world's leading independent think tank for international economics. Over his career, Adam has contributed to research and public policy regarding monetary and fiscal policies in the G20, the challenges of European integration since the adoption of the euro, China–US economic relations, and developing new approaches to financial recovery and stability.

Ambassador J. Stapleton Roy is the Founding Director Emeritus and a Distinguished Scholar at the Wilson Center's Kissinger Institute on China and the United States. He was born in China, speaks fluent Mandarin, and has spent his life studying the development of the country. J. Stapleton Roy holds the rank of Career Ambassador and has served as the top US envoy to Singapore, China, and Indonesia. After retiring from the State Department, he went on to head the newly created Kissinger Institute on China and the United States at the Wilson Center.

John L. Thornton is the Chair Emeritus of the Brookings Institution and Co-Chair of The Asia Society. Thornton has had a distinguished career in finance. He is currently Executive Chairman of Barrick Gold and Chairman of PineBridge Investments and was previously President of Goldman Sachs. Thornton has a long-standing relationship with China and is Professor and Director of global leadership at Tsinghua University.

For this dialogue, we were also joined by CCG Advisor Zhu Guangyao. Zhu was a former Vice Minister at China's Ministry of Finance, where he

G. Zhu
Counsellor's Office of the State Council, Beijing, China

oversaw the Customs Tariff Department and helped to coordinate the economic track of the China–US Strategic and Economic Dialogue. He also works for a think tank under the Ministry of Finance.

This dialogue took place approximately six months into Biden's presidency, shortly after US Deputy Secretary of State Wendy Sherman visited China and Ambassador Qin Gang, the new Chinese envoy to the US, arrived in Washington. The representatives of Chinese and US think tanks began by sharing their views on the current state of China–US relations and went on to have a wide-ranging discussion covering economic ties, political factors shaping the bilateral relationship, the need for cooperation to address shared global challenges, economic integration through vehicles such as the WTO and CPTPP, and the importance of maintaining people-to-people ties between the two countries.

Huiyao Wang: I'm very pleased to be able to host this dialogue between Chinese and US think tanks tonight. I would like to start with Adam. What are your thoughts on the US and Chinese economy and how we get out of this pandemic, US–China relations, and trade?

Adam S. Posen: I think the big message on the questions you raise is that US–China frictions are not about economics, even though they currently take place in economics. This has been a major preoccupation under Trump and again under Biden. As I argued in my recent article in *Foreign Affairs* titled "The Price of Nostalgia," [current frictions] are mostly being driven by politics in both China and the US, where basically the males working in industry in non-urban centers are blackmailing the rest of society. And we see this with the state-owned enterprises in China, we see this with the trade bailouts of heavy industry in the US. In both countries, those parts of the economy are the shrinking part of the economy and a shrinking part of employment. They also are industries that are toxic to our environment as well as to our politics.

So, what we are seeing is that both the American and Chinese peoples are being ill-served by the trade conflict. It's not about economics. What we've seen under the Biden administration, partly of its own initiative and partly in response to the Xi government, is a shift now from trade to worrying about technology. Obviously, there have been frictions for many years, and others on this panel have been dealing with them directly for even longer than I have, over issues of intellectual property and government subsidies. But for the most part, these have not been issues that should have imperiled the broader relationship on an economic basis.

What has escalated it now is the sense in the US and China that [the other country] poses a genuine threat, in the geopolitical sense, and in a sense a threat to their system or their legitimacy. This is now a reality among the official class in both Washington and Beijing. There's some good reason for [this view], but it's mostly exaggerated, and it colors every interaction. So, the question is, what can we do from here? Let me make three very brief points, so you can get to the others on the panel.

First, remember that both the US and China have led the world in recovery from the COVID crisis and are now both growing above-trend growth rates by a large margin. So, this is not a question of either country depriving the other of economic recovery. There is no conflict over currency right now. There is no issue of Chinese [trade] surpluses coming at US expense. There is no issue of financial instability being promoted from one to the other or back and forth. So, we have to focus on the non-economic issues, which is funny for an economist like me to say.

Second, the biggest opportunity for collaboration between China and the US is on climate change issues. That was the case under President Obama when our friend Minister Zhu was very active in the G7 and the G20, and that remains the best place for us to collaborate at this time.

Third, since you were generous enough to convene a group of think tankers, I just want to say that we—CCG, the Peterson Institute, Brookings, the Kissinger Center, and the Ministry of Finance's own think tank—all have a role in continuing to say that we should not be afraid of honest dialogue among experts. We have a common enemy in conspiracy theories and disinformation. We think tanks should be binding ourselves together to emphasize the possibility of objective analysis and honest, frank talk. Thank you very much for this opportunity.

Huiyao Wang: Thank you, Adam. I agree it seems that now economic issues have deterred us from talking of things of real substance at a time when we need to collaborate on addressing the pandemic, climate change, and many other things.

Now, let's have some opening remarks from Ambassador Roy. As a seasoned diplomat that has known China since childhood, what is your take on the past, present, and future of China–US relations? This year is the 50th anniversary of Kissinger's visit to China. We recently had a dialogue with Dr. Kissinger to mark this event and your institute [the Kissinger Institute on China and the United States] at the Wilson Center is named after him. This year also marks 50 years since the People's

Republic of China resumed its membership in the UN, 20 years since joining the WTO, and 30 years since joining APEC. So, there are lots of reminders of the past this year.

J. Stapleton Roy: Thank you Dr. Wang and good evening to all of you who are in China. When President Trump lost the November 2020 presidential elections in the US, some people hoped that President Biden would adopt a less confrontational approach to relations with China. They have been disappointed. Early steps by the new American administration toward China seemed to be a continuation of President Trump's hardline policies. Shortly after the administration took office, the new Secretary of State echoed the charge of his predecessor that China was engaged in genocide against the Uighurs in Xinjiang. The tariff barriers on bilateral trade have been left in place. Senior officials in the Biden administration bluntly stated that US engagement strategies toward China had failed and that competition is now the principal driver in the bilateral relationship.

For much of the last 50 years, the US was confident that China's growing wealth and power did not threaten the vital interests of the United States and that their differences could be managed by diplomacy and engagement. That is no longer the case. The question is why.

A starting point to understanding what has happened is to recognize that the US and China are both in the midst of fundamental transitions that affect their respective places in the world. The US is seeking to adjust to an international situation in which it is no longer the sole superpower. This is not so much because of a decline in power, but because other countries have risen to major power status. China, of course, is the first and foremost example of that. A new multipolar world is emerging. Not surprisingly, the US is reluctant to give up the dominant position that it has occupied since the end of the Cold War and to accept the adjustments that it must make in order to establish a new equilibrium. At the same time, there is no question that the social and political polarization that has been a prominent feature of the US domestic scene over the last half-decade has damaged the international image of the US and the perception of its reliability as a great power.

China, in turn, in a remarkably short period of time, has regained the wealth and military strength that are the attributes of major powers. This has altered the psychology of the Chinese people. This is what Zheng Bijian didn't take into account when he came up with the concept of "peaceful rise." The Chinese people now are demanding a more muscular foreign policy consistent with China's growing power. This has changed

Chinese behavior patterns, which have become more assertive. As a result, regional countries, including the US, find less and less credible China's assurances that it will rise peacefully and never bully its neighbors.

These are two of the key background factors that have influenced the sharp plunge in the bilateral US–China relationship to the lowest depths in half a century. This has created a dangerous situation where missteps by either side or by both could plunge the world into an unprecedented crisis. I use the term "unprecedented" because China and the US are both major nuclear powers, making confrontations between them particularly dangerous.

Repair work by both sides is vitally necessary. Fortunately, despite some superficial similarities, the Biden administration is fundamentally different from its predecessor. President Biden has more foreign policy and national security experience than any American president since the first President Bush 30 years ago. In contrast to the Trump Administration, President Biden has appointed capable and experienced officials as secretary of state and national security advisor. These are officials who could sit down without talking points and talk for hours with Chinese counterparts about any issue in the world. This was totally missing in the last administration. The Biden administration is moving carefully to iron out internal differences and adopt sustainable policies that will not simply reflect the whims of one man. Of particular importance for US–China Relations, the administration has reaffirmed that it will adhere to the One-China policy and that it does not support independence for Taiwan. It is also seeking a pattern of regular consultations between Beijing and Washington.

The recent consultations between US Deputy Secretary of State Wendy Sherman and State Councilor and Foreign Minister Wang Yi, together with Vice Minister Xie Feng [in July 2021], were surrounded by a barrage of charges by each side against the other. However, if one reads carefully the public reports regarding the consultations, it is evident that there were constructive elements. According to the Chinese account of the meeting, Deputy Secretary Sherman called the US–China relationship "the most important bilateral relationship in the world," noted the many times that the two sides have had contact with each other since President Biden was sworn in, expressed US' willingness to have open and candid contacts and dialogues with China, declared that the US' hopes that the two countries could coexist peacefully, said that the US has no intention of restricting Chinese development, and affirmed that the US does not want to contain China and would like to see China develop further. [She also] noted that the two sides could engage in healthy competition, cooperate on climate change, drug control, and international and regional hotspots, strengthen crisis management capacity, and avoid conflicts. American accounts of the meetings are consistent with the above statements. These are encouraging words that you would not have heard from the previous administration.

However, the reality is less positive. President Biden needs congressional support for his domestic programs, and congressional attitudes toward China are hostile. Changing these attitudes will be difficult but not impossible. A hardline American approach to China does not mesh well with the interests of US allies and friends in East Asia, who do not wish to see the region polarized. In other words, a US that tries to work with our friends and allies will discover that they do not support a hardline approach to China. I think that will have an impact over time. But as the first step, it would be useful for both China and the US to tone down their rhetoric toward each other. Governments have the responsibility not only to formulate wise foreign policies, but also to talk in ways that develop public support for those policies. We are not doing that. We are talking publicly in ways that undermine the wise policy that we should be pursuing. So as a starter, let's get our rhetoric under control. I hope that we'll have some chance to exchange views about other steps that could be taken.

Huiyao Wang: Thank you, I agree that it's a deep concern on both sides that we seem to argue and quarrel with each other all the time. Trump has done quite a lot of damage to existing relations. One of the problems with the Trump administration was that its core team was not that savvy on China. In contrast, President Biden has a lot of knowledge of foreign policy, as you said, and has spent more time with President Xi than perhaps any other leader in the world.

Now I'd like to invite Minister Zhu who is a CCG advisor and works for the think tank of the Ministry of Finance. As an expert on China–US relations that previously led the Strategic and Economic Dialogue and served as a shepherd for the G20, what's your take on this issue?

Zhu Guangyao: Thank you very much. I'll try my best to discuss and give some responses to the points from Adam and Ambassador Roy.

Unfortunately, as described, China–US relations are now at a critical juncture, and I think the big issue is mutual trust. As Adam said, it's something that goes beyond economics. As two important countries, we must maintain communications, increase our understanding of each other, and try our best to restore mutual trust. I know this is not easy to do, but I still think that economic ties are the anchor for our bilateral relationship. Last year, China–US trade volume reached $580 billion and in the first half of this year, that number increased more than 50 percent year on year, reaching $340 billion. So, despite political pressure and negative public opinion on both sides, we see trade still increasing, which is a good thing, because our integrated economies have also closely connected our interests. I agree with Adam that trade tariffs and the technology war have had a very negative impact. Now, it is important to restore basic communication.

Ambassador Roy mentioned that the Biden administration's team is professional, which I agree with, as I used to deal with many of the officials in Biden's team. But I must point out some key issues that the Biden administration should correct immediately since it is in the US interest. This includes tariffs, which as [US Treasury] Secretary Yellen said, are not in US interests and harm US consumers. However, six months have now passed and there hasn't been any single change. On the political side, Ambassador Roy mentioned the genocide issue, which was absolutely a wrong judgment made by the last administration in its last two weeks in office. They used this as a reason to block the import of all cotton and tomatoes produced in Xinjiang. Unfortunately, Biden's Secretary of State has adhered to the previous policy and continued to claim that in Xinjiang there is genocide of Uighurs. This kind of standpoint is definitely wrong and creates danger in China–US relations—in Ambassador Roy's words, "an unprecedented risk."

Adam raised some points which I think are very important. The first was that [current frictions are] something beyond the economic situation. Yes, we should have more a comprehensive discussion and find a way to expand our discussion beyond the economy. Also, I think that everything is connected in terms of economic relations because US entrepreneurs need a good environment for their investments in China, and likewise for Chinese investments in the US. Second, climate change is certainly a practical way forward for cooperation, including environment, social, and governance (ESG). I think this has already become broader than just the climate change issue. Think tanks can also be a real channel for cooperation.

In this regard, I have four points or suggestions. The first is that China and the US must find ways to deal with our challenges and develop peaceful coexistence. Based on communication and mutual understanding, we should enhance our cooperation to realize peaceful coexistence. Second, both China and the US need to keep on opening and reforming. China is deepening its structural reform and opening to the outside world—for our own domestic interests, of course—and this is also in line with global cooperation. The third point is we must have real cooperation on our multilateral system for trade and financial institutions, the WHO, the IMF, the World Bank, and other UN special agencies. We need to maintain and enhance this network of global institutions to ensure continued peace and development.

The last suggestion is that for effective dialogue and communication, we need real mechanisms such as the S&ED (US–China Strategic and Economic Dialogue) and the BIT (US–China Bilateral Investment Treaty), on which I participated in negotiations under the Obama administration and is now 90 percent finished. The most important issue that has not been resolved is the digital economy, including data flows across the world and data privacy issues, which have become more important today. The US, China, the EU, and others are emphasizing domestically how important the development of the digital economy is while enhancing security and privacy. Addressing these issues requires global action and global negotiations. One possible breakthrough could come with e-commerce negotiations in the WTO. It will be difficult, but we should try, for the sake of future growth and cooperation between China and the US.

Huiyao Wang: Thank you, Minister Zhu, you raised many good points. Now I would like to invite John Thornton to comment. During last year's CCG Annual Forum, you talked about the deficit of trust between the US and China and how we can build up the trust. Now we are half a year into the new Biden administration, what more can be done? John, you have the floor, please.

John Thornton: Thank you Henry and thank you for inviting me to participate in this very interesting and important dialogue. I'm honored to be a member of this particular panel. We've already heard quite a bit of wisdom from my three colleagues and I will try to make a modest contribution. What I'd like to do is to step back from the breathless statements of doom, which dominate much of the immediate commentary in the media, among politicians, and among so-called experts, or even the thoughtful observations of concern, which may be overly influenced by specific current actions by one party or the other.

The US–China relationship is and will be both the most important bilateral relationship of this century, and the one which will drive or create in large measure the world in which we all will live. In general, I am skeptical of the statements about "inflection points" or "decoupling" or Cold War analogies. For me, these kinds of statements are mostly emotional, provocative, not helpful, and wrong. I think we're better off looking at the long-term trajectory and the dynamics, trends, and forces creating that long-term.

Recently, I have taken to looking at the mid-twenty-first century, the year 2050 or thereabouts. The best estimates are that the world's population in 2050 will be about 10 billion people. Today we are approximately 7.8 billion. Of the incremental 2.2 billion, more than half will come from nine countries: India, Nigeria, the Democratic Republic of the Congo, Pakistan, Ethiopia, Tanzania, the US, Uganda, and Indonesia. In 2050, as now, a small percentage of the world's countries will represent 65–70 percent of the global GDP—maybe the top 10 countries will represent that [share]. In that world in which very few countries dominate the global GDP, and in which the incremental 2 plus billion people come from very poor countries, does any serious thinking person believe the world would be better off with the rich countries primarily arguing or even fighting amongst themselves, while the rest of the vast percentage of the world remains poor, malnourished, victims of climate change, and sources of migration, disease, and poverty? Or do the wealthy, most powerful countries have a responsibility to work together to lead the world to a safer, more prosperous, harmonious place? Isn't the answer obvious? If the answer is so obvious, then why does it feel or seem that at least some, maybe many, of the world's richest and most powerful countries do not seem to be animated or motivated by such a collective goal?

There are a myriad of answers to this question, but it certainly includes a penchant for being captured or trapped by the past and old ways of thinking, as well as a fear of change, of losing one's place. Whatever the reasons, surely the world's two most powerful countries, the US and China, have a disproportionate responsibility to lead the world, of course, with others. There is no reason why they cannot do this. In fact, we have a unique asset at this very moment in history, which we have never had before. The newly elected US President Joe Biden has a pre-existing relationship with the Chinese President Xi Jinping. When President Biden and Xi were vice presidents of their countries, they spent extensive, continuous, informal time with one another, probably more genuine private time than any two US and Chinese presidents have ever spent with one another. This is a gift from providence. We cannot throw this asset away. Indeed, we must use it to its fullest extent.

Knowing the two presidents, Biden and Xi, as people, as human beings, as leaders, does anyone think that a well-conceived meeting, one on one, between the two of them, would be anything other than a strong, good, healthy, warm, and productive meeting? Knowing what we know about the two countries and their positions in the world, does anyone think such a good meeting would not be well-received by the American and Chinese people, or by people all over the world? Of course, it would. This is not that difficult, and there is a screamingly obvious place to start: climate change in the G20 meeting in Rome.

The issue of climate is a global one; it is larger and more important than the US and China. The entire thinking world wants it to be solved or well-managed. The two leading countries must lead on the solution or it will not be solved. Everyone knows this. Tellingly, the two presidents are following the only path, the only modus operandi, that works in US–China relations; one might call this the Zhou Enlai-Kissinger model, or, more recently, the Liu He-Lighthizer model. The only model that we know works is when the US and Chinese presidents appoint a very senior, serious, experienced, and highly trusted individual, and together the two presidents instruct the two people to get into a metaphysical room, truly work together, build a relationship of trust, and not to come out until they have solved the problem. The two presidents have done just that with the appointment of John Kerry and Xie Zhenhua [as climate envoys]. Meanwhile, it would be helpful while the two are doing their work if the two sides moderated their language about all other matters. Or as [J. Stapleton Roy] said, "tone down the rhetoric."

By definition, no other matter is as important as the existence of the planet. Mankind has to exist for all other matters to have an opportunity to flourish and or be addressed. This is a point of simple compelling priority. Both presidents have publicly said that they will cooperate on climate irrespective of other issues. Both should instruct their senior leaders to give the existential issue a real chance to get resolved. Finally, to state the obvious, success on climate will demonstrate yet again that the US and China working together can lead the world to a better safer, healthier, more harmonious existence. This is good for both countries and the world and gives hope and a concrete model, that all other gnarly complex problems can likewise be addressed by the two leading countries working together with others for the collective benefit of their countries, their peoples, and the world. Thank you.

Huiyao Wang: Thank you very much, John, you have outlined an excellent proposal. I agree that the relationship between China and the US is the most important in the world and that we must work together on many issues, given that the world is going through the profound changes you mentioned.

I have a follow-up question, since you are part of the investment community and led Goldman Sachs for many years. As you said, developing countries are going to see a lot of population growth and many lack adequate infrastructure. During this [2021] CCG annual forum, former Vice Minister of Commerce Chen Jian, who looked after Chinese outbound investment for many years, said there is scope for cooperation between the B3W proposed at the G7 conference [in June 2021], the BRI, and EU infrastructure investment plans. Recently, President Xi had a video conference with French President Macron and German Chancellor Angela Merkel [in July 2021] when they talked about China–EU collaboration in Africa. What do you think about opportunities for cooperation?

John Thornton: First of all, I want to remind people that when the BRI was first conceived back in 2013. There was a G20 meeting and President Xi met with a very senior American who was standing in for President Obama as President Obama was not present. In that meeting, President Xi told the Americans about the concept he had for the BRI. The senior American said to President Xi, "What a fantastic idea, maybe we can do this together?" And President Xi said, "That would be an excellent idea, let's do it together." The senior American went back to the US and in the next six months or so, the Mandarin technicians decided it wasn't a good idea, and the idea got killed in the US before it ever got to President Obama's desk, and so the cooperation never occurred. Since then, as you know, the BRI has been characterized by many people in the US as some kind of nefarious geostrategic plan to take over the world, which it's not.

To your question, of course, the B3W, BRI, and similar efforts should be coordinated globally by the wealthy countries to build the infrastructure necessary for the rest of the world, so that we build a safer, more prosperous world. We all know these projects are very difficult to execute, it's not as though anyone's got a monopoly on how to do this well.

They are hard. We would be doing ourselves a great service if we, the world, became expert at building important infrastructure in an efficient manner for the benefit of countries across the world. So obviously we should [cooperate on infrastructure], there's no question about that.

Huiyao Wang: After the first round of discussion, allow me to come back to our other distinguished panelists. Adam, I know the Peterson Institute has been studying the Trans-Pacific Partnership (TPP) for many years. When President Trump withdrew the US from the TPP, CCG *was the first think tank* in China to propose that China should join TPP. We issued several reports on this topic and have constantly been advocating for [China to join].

Premier Li mentioned at last year's National People's Congress [in May 2020] that China is interested in joining CPTPP and President Xi announced at the APEC summit that China will "actively consider" joining CPTPP. Given PIIE's expertise on this topic, what is your take on CPTPP? Its rules cover issues such as data flow, IPR protection, environmental protection, labor standards, SOE reform, and comparative neutrality. The US designed the TPP [the predecessor to CPTPP], so why doesn't Washington come back to the table to talk about these important issues? Building on this foundation, maybe the US and China could promote reforms of the WTO based on experience in regional integration through agreements like RCEP, CPTPP, and others. Adam, your take, please.

Adam S. Posen: Let me pick up on what you and Minister Zhu were saying about reform. The most important thing about CPTPP, especially as it has evolved since President Trump withdrew, is that it is a high-standard agreement and it is an open agreement. As you say, the Peterson Institute has been doing work on economic agreements and free trade areas, particularly in Asia, for decades. Previously, there was a debate between my predecessor, Fred Bergsten, and the distinguished Columbia economist Jagdish Bhagwati about trade blocs—"stumbling blocks" versus "building blocks." The basic message that we took, that I have altered slightly, is that regional agreements can be useful if they genuinely open things up and if they genuinely encourage reform and high standards in the countries that are members, and if you are not biasing them by political factors. So, I'm going to go out on an unusual limb here and say, for the time being, it would be good if CPTPP continues to succeed and grow without either China or the US being involved.

In the current context, there are a number of people in both the Chinese and American governments looking to line up various developing countries around the world, including but not solely in East and South Asia, as being on one side or the other. This relates to what Professor Thornton was saying about the BRI. I think it was very good to have a live, high-standard, open entity that is neither Chinese nor American, something that offers a way forward without asking people to commit to one side or another in some sense. We can see this in the extension of CPTPP, potentially to the UK and to Korea. In both cases, this would send an important message to the rest of the world—that you can have high-standard commerce on the issues you raised, including labor rights, environmental standards, data privacy, state subsidies, and so on, all the things that the Obama administration and former US Trade Representative Mike Froman argued for, but also the Japanese, Singaporean, Australian, and New Zealand governments. That can be a standard that then puts pressure on both the US and China to raise their own games. This goes with something I wrote almost a year ago, where I encouraged the Australians and the Japanese to pursue what I call "principled plurilateralism"—that is, they should be willing to engage in these plurilateral deals, but the deals have to be based on quality and standards.

I think this will disappoint some people in both Beijing and Washington, particularly in Washington, where the arguments for [TPP] initially and to now bring CPTPP back to Washington are all about aligning the trading system against China or having a bloc that puts pressure on China by exclusion. I also think that it's preferable to go this route, having an independent strong CPTPP that's not dominated by China or the US, because, frankly, we know that once trade agreements are made, you'd have issues of enforcement, and China and the US would probably make as conditions of their accession changes to the CPTPP or changes to enforcement. It will not be entirely reliable; we've seen this in the way the US has repeatedly renegotiated the USMCA and the US–Korea trade agreement. We've seen this in other ways in China's deals.

If we keep it open to everyone but China and the US, without saying so, CPTPP is big enough that anybody who accedes, including South Korea or the UK, would have to be an accession country. Now, my friend Zhu Guangyao mentions the importance of multilateral institutions, and obviously, the WTO is lurking in the background here. I think there are ways of keeping [principled plurilateralism] compatible with the WTO, but plurilateral deals "of the willing" are necessary to keep moving reform forward; we cannot have India and Brazil blocking all progress on trade. Though I should put in one footnote—the above view [about CPTPP] is not Peterson Institute's position, it is my own.

The final point I would make, in light of Guangyao and Stapleton Roy rightly raising this point, is that the pandemic response is far more important than any other thing we have talked about [...] The world is incredibly divided, with the poor countries being excluded from vaccine distribution and likely to suffer for a long time, both economically and socially. This isn't just about public health, this has much more long-lasting implications.

I think a CPTPP with China and/or the US would reinforce the message to the rich countries or the countries already integrated, that they can get on with their business and ignore what happens in the rest of the world. That message is already coming through strongly on the vaccination and aid front. So, at this time, I would much rather see China and the US put their efforts into being helpful [with pandemic response] rather than into CPTPP. I want Japan, Australia, Singapore, Canada, and all the members of CPTPP to move forward, but not China and the US.

Huiyao Wang: So, you mean that we should let CPTPP run for a while and experiment with that. But what about the WTO? The WTO Ministerial Conference is coming up this year and we have a new director-general in post.[1] What do you think of the prospects for WTO reform? We have these plurilateral meetings for the digital economy and trade and investment facilitation. Also, the G7 and OECD have proposed a global minimum corporate tax, to which China is one of the 130 countries that has agreed. How can bodies like the G20 turn their efforts to fighting the pandemic and addressing economic issues?

Adam S. Posen: On the WTO, as with so many things, the rhetoric has outstripped the reality. All the talk about WTO reform and WTO dysfunction, especially in Washington, is exaggerated and unjustified. I think the frustrations with large-scale trade rounds are real and there are some tweaks to be had to the WTO body. But the new Director-General Ngozi Okonjo-Iweala, who I admire greatly, has come in with the right attitude, which is don't try to fix everything at once, don't get caught up in procedures, try to get deliverables, and show the world that the WTO

---

[1] At the time of this discussion, this meeting was scheduled for November 2021, but was later postponed due to COVID-19.

can deliver things that matter to people. She is rightly focusing on trade issues, dealing with the pandemic, fisheries, and direct limited appellate body reforms. I think this is the right way to go. There are too many things to be done. What's important is that the WTO leadership gets the membership, in time for the end of this year's Ministerial Conference, to make meaningful progress on two or three of these issues. One is the pandemic, otherwise, it doesn't matter which of the [other] issues, you just need to demonstrate that the WTO can do something useful. I think if we go off in too many directions at once, it's not going to be helpful.

On a minimum corporate tax, it was wonderful to see China and other major economies agree on this. I think it is critically important for the legitimacy of taxation in all societies, as well as providing revenues on a stable basis for all societies, that we get the international corporations, notably but not solely the US digital giants, under this regime and to not have base erosion and profit shifting. Again, Minister Zhu was involved in the first rounds of those discussions, and I praise him and I praise [US Treasury] Secretary Yellen for leading us. My fear, speaking frankly, is that this may be a repeat "League of Nations moment." [...] You have a progressive Democrat, the American leadership gets agreement on something at the global level and comes back and finds an isolationist Republican US Senate prevents it from being enacted, and then the world has to go forward somehow, without the US participating. I think it could be disastrous if the US Congress does not take up what the US Treasury Secretary rightly negotiated on behalf of the US and the world.

The second point [about the global corporate minimum tax] is that it's not perfect, going back to the themes we've all hit. This was an OECD agreement because that's where the multinationals are and that's where the expertise was, and it makes sense. But as my colleagues Gary Hufbauer and Simeon Djankov have written for the Peterson Institute, there are a lot of small countries in the world that are not purely tax havens, that are not Ireland or the Netherlands, that are going to be affected by this development. Again, it's wonderful to see China and the US willing to cooperate on something substantive, but there has to be some engagement of the needs of developing countries and small countries. So, it's not a done deal. My biggest fear, as I said, is the US [...] doing the right thing internationally and failing to deliver domestically.

Huiyao Wang: Thank you, Adam. I think, particularly, China's accepting the G20 proposal for a global minimum tax is really a good sign. If we do sit down and really analyze the global economic situation, we can collaborate.

Ambassador Roy—you are a seasoned diplomat and spent many years in China, including during your childhood. I still vividly remember a few years back when we went to Dunhuang together and then when you accompanied us to visit Seattle in the US. After four decades of engagement between the US in China, some in the US are now saying, "China has not converged with us, has not become one of us." But China has 5000 years of history and its own development path. Given your experience in China, how do you see future developments between China and the US?

J. Stapleton Roy: I referred in my opening remarks to the fact that the US was having difficulty adjusting to the need for a new equilibrium in East Asia. I think that's a real problem for us. If you read American speeches and writings on the subject, we still have many people who think that dominance in air and naval power, for example, is necessary for the US. You can't have a new equilibrium if either China or the US is setting dominance as a goal because the other side will not accept it. Therefore, if we're going to have a dialogue with China, we have to begin addressing the question of how to strike a military balance in which each country feels it can meet its defense needs—for the US, that includes the defense needs of our allies—but is not so powerful that we appear to have the capability to engage in aggression against the other side. We are not yet there, and we are not yet mentally prepared to try to undertake that task, and it is absolutely necessary. Because you have to have a balance of power in East Asia; otherwise we're going to be continually in strategic rivalry with each other. That's one reason why I think it is absolutely wrong to think that [the dominant factor in the bilateral relationship] has to be strategic rivalry. Because strategic rivalry always focuses on the military component and that ends up generating an endless arms race in which resources are diverted away from economic development into military development.

I think the US has to stop thinking in terms of "dominance" and I think the Biden administration was wrong when it introduced the concept of "dealing with China from a position of strength." Anybody would understand that China would never accept that as a basis for the US to deal with China. The same term cropped up during the Cold War when I worked on Soviet affairs. The Soviets were very sensitive to the idea of the US dealing with them "from a position of strength."

But China is making an enormous mistake by not defining its defense needs strictly in terms of China's defense requirements. Now, China has linked its defense needs to its international status as a great power. At the 18th Party Congress in 2012, the first part of the military portion of the work report talked about China needing a powerful military commensurate with its international standing and appropriate for its defense and development needs. At the 19th Party Congress, [the work report] talked about requiring a "world-class" military power. Well, if China has a world-class military power when it has no global military responsibilities—China has no allies beyond its immediate periphery in which it has the military capability to meet those requirements—so when Americans look at China, we don't see any ceiling in terms of where China wants to develop its military power. In my opinion, China has to rethink how it is talking about its military requirements. Because if every country tries to develop military capabilities in terms of their international status, what size of military does Japan need? What size of military does India need, et cetera? It's the wrong way of looking at the issue.

Military requirements should be linked to defense requirements. The US and China need to be thinking in terms of, as President Xi himself has said, "a Pacific in which China and US can both function together." Xi said the Pacific is large enough for both China and the US. In his earlier speeches, Xi has specifically referred to the defense dilemma, which is that if China has absolute security, then its neighbors have no security. He has used that exact language in his speeches, so he understands the issue—that there has to be a limit on China's defense capabilities, or its neighbors will all lack security. This is an area where the US and China, sooner or later (and the sooner the better), need to start engaging in a dialogue to see if there is a possibility for a strategic equilibrium in East Asia that is compatible with the national interests of both sides. And that means that national interests also have to be defined in a way that doesn't exclude that possibility.

So, I think there is enormous scope for China and the US to stop looking at the world in terms of their own domestic driving factors. I understand that they have to look at the external circumstances in the world in an objective way and then formulate foreign policies that are compatible with the international circumstances in which they have to operate. And they each have to gain domestic support for that approach. The US is not yet doing that. For example, if we look at East Asia, where all of the countries of East Asia have more trade with China than with the US, it is clear that if we ask Asian countries to choose between China and the US, they are not going to want to do so, because they have very important interests with China. So, we have to understand that in our foreign policy approach to China, and in the way we talk about China, we must not describe our approach in ways that require countries to choose between the "good" US with our democratic system and the "bad" China with its authoritarian system—that's the wrong way to formulate our foreign policy concepts.

China, as I've already illustrated, in my judgment is making the same mistake as it is talking about needing global military power because of its status as a great power. Going back to the nineteenth century, when China talked about the need for China to regain "wealth and power," the power was so that China would no longer be the object of aggression by stronger countries. It was a defensive concept, not an aggressive concept. That has been lost now because China is talking about how a powerful military is needed because of its international standing. So, this is an area where I think both of our countries need to do a lot more serious thinking.

Huiyao Wang: Thank you, Ambassador Roy, you explained really well that countries should not use ideology or outdated mindsets to assess twenty-first-century realities. We need a new narrative, and you are right that we should not seek dominance over each other.

Minister Zhu, I remember in 2016 at the Hangzhou G20, you were the G20 coordinator for the Ministry of Finance. I saw an interview with you on CCTV shot next to West Lake in Hangzhou when you were saying that the BIT was almost agreed between China and the US. Another story I heard you tell is how during the 2008 financial crisis, you had a call from the US Treasury office on how China and the US could work together to deal with the crisis, after which China launched a CNY 4 trillion revival plan. At that time, the US and China worked together through the crisis. What do you think about this current crisis amidst the pandemic, how can we work together?

Zhu Guangyao: Before I answer your question, I just want to respond to Ambassador Roy's idea regarding military strategy and military intention. To be honest, in modern history, China has suffered a lot from foreign invasions. The Chinese people deeply understand that, so it's the peoples' willingness that China becomes a stronger country. However, for strategy and the real situation, when China talks about its core interests, it's always three points. One, sovereignty, two, territorial integrity, and three, the right to development. We hope that China can become a modernized socialist country, a united country, and a country that can improve people's living standards.

Regarding the 2016 G20 meeting and the China–US BIT talks, which occurred under the strong leadership of President Xi Jinping and President Obama. Before the G20 Hangzhou Summit, the Chinese team and the US team worked very hard. The leader of the US team [US Trade Representative], Michael Froman, maintained very close communications with the Chinese team, nearly every day, sometimes even three or four times a day. At that time, we could say publicly that the BIT was nearly 90 percent complete. We understood that some key challenges remained on the digital economy, particularly data privacy and movement of data across borders, and we just needed more hard work to address these. Unfortunately, as we know, the US administration then changed and even abandoned TPP, which delayed the continuation of negotiations.

Another case was in 2008. I remember that during the international financial crisis, in October 2008, at 3 a.m. in the morning, I received a phone call from my counterpart in the US Treasury. She immediately arranged a meeting between Treasury Secretary Hank Paulson and his Chinese counterpart to talk about the possible upgrading of the G20 format from being between finance ministers and central bank governors to national leaders. I think it was around 10 a.m. Beijing time, and we [resolved to do this] over a three or four-hour phone call, which really forged the path for the G20 summit in November in Washington DC, chaired by President Bush and joined by Chinese President Hu. That was a very successful meeting that paved the way for the next G20 meeting in London to build up a real firewall for the IMF, where we struck a deal to pool one trillion US dollars to face the challenge of the international financial crisis. That really demonstrated what a positive impact China–US cooperation can have.

Huiyao Wang: Thank you, Minister Zhu. We should draw lessons from our cooperation in tackling the global financial crisis. We could really use that spirit to fight the current pandemic as well.

At the end of this second round of discussion, I'd like to ask John to comment. You've taught at Tsinghua University's Economics and Management School for many years, have served as an honorary chair of Brookings Institution for over a decade, and have been with the Asia Society in the US for several years. Currently, there is an issue with student exchanges between China and US. I heard that the US Embassy is issuing 1000 visas a day and that by the end of summer, it is going to issue

200,000 visas for Chinese students going to the US. But looking at the numbers, there is still a refusal rate of about 2 or 3 percent.

How do you think we can promote people-to-people exchange, business exchange, tourism, cultural exchange, and of course, exchange between think tanks during this special time? How can we work with travel bans, as we are probably going to have to live with this virus for a long time?

John Thornton: Thank you, Henry, I can be succinct on this point. To state the obvious, the ties between American and Chinese people are absolutely essential to getting the relationship where it needs to be. I'm hopeful that the younger people who have a vested interest in the long-term future of their countries and the world will be forces for good in the relationship. One way of thinking about China, for example, is to think about the roughly 400 million millennials, how they have grown up, and how they think about the future. The Chinese leadership needs to be responsive to that group. And the same thing is true in the US. The ties between those groups are absolutely central to forward progress and I'm pleased to see that this is one area where [the Biden administration] is moving quickly to rectify the policy of the previous administration, to open back up again, and to support people-to-people exchange. We all know that the ties are deep and broad, they are state-to-state, universities-to-universities, NGOs-to-NGOs, individuals-to-individuals. It cannot be overstated, the sort of societal trust that needs to be built, was being built, and can be built. This is probably the single best insurance policy against untoward policy on the part of the leadership. I think in some ways, the wisdom or common sense of ordinary people can act as a kind of a break against the occasional unwise policies of elites.

Huiyao Wang: Thank you. We've had a very good discussion today. During our final round of concluding remarks, maybe you can add any further thoughts on our theme of "balanced competition and cooperation."

Adam S. Posen: It's been such a rich discussion, and you gave me plenty of opportunities to speak. All I would say is that as we're trying to balance competition and cooperation, the key point for both countries, or at least both economies, is to allow for some openness and allow the businesses, people, and scholars to cooperate, even if the governments choose to compete. We know from history, including the McCarthy era and parts of the Cold War in the US, that when societies close down, they create their own corruption and their own abuse of power, as well as the obvious economic and human costs. I think this is where the think tanks, to the extent that we are allowed to do so, have to be out there reminding people that even if the top government officials in Washington and Beijing want to emphasize the competition, that usually gets distorted into abuse of power internally in those countries, and we should be calling people out on that.

Huiyao Wang: Good. Ambassador Roy?

J. Stapleton Roy: I think the visit to Beijing by Dr. Kissinger 50 years ago is well worth commemorating. Because it illustrated that when national interest is served by cooperation, differences in political and social systems do not have to block that cooperation. The problem with differences in systems, which has become a big issue in the US in terms of thinking about China, is that at some level, it does influence cooperation, but it shouldn't block it if it's in the national interest to cooperate. The problem is illustrated by our ability to cooperate with Joseph Stalin when we were opposing Hitler. But when Hitler had been defeated, our ability to cooperate with the Soviet Union broke down. So, in some ways, that's the type of issue we face with China.

There are forces in the US that want to block our cooperation with China because of the differences in our political systems. We need to remember the Nixon and Kissinger opening to China at a time when there couldn't have been bigger differences between our domestic systems. China was at the height of the Cultural Revolution when that occurred, and yet we set that aside because of the importance of cooperating with China against the Soviet threat. In my judgment, if we look at what the world requires, and at our responsibilities as great nations, it is clear to me that the lesson of Kissinger's visit to China is that when it is necessary to have cooperation between China and the US, we should not let the differences in our systems block that type of cooperation. So, I think it was a very important visit. Historically, it created the possibilities for the US and China to create enormous common interests, and those common interests, in my judgment, continue and we have to find ways to cooperate in promoting them.

Huiyao Wang: Thank you, Ambassador Roy. So, Minister Zhu—your concluding remarks.

Zhu Guangyao: Thank you Huiyao. Today's situation and the relationship between China and the US is something different from that of 50 years ago. One key point is that the Chinese and American economies are so closely connected. Not only is there more than $500 billion in bilateral trade each year, but also investment, and coordination on global governance.

However, we also face new challenges with domestic public opinion, such as populism in both America and China. At this time, we really need strong leadership from the two presidents. I think that we must follow the spirit that President Xi and President Biden embraced during their conversation on the eve of Chinese New Year. Just as Ambassador Roy said, we should expand our common ground and make our cooperation broader. As John said, we also need to enhance interactions between our two societies, including academic and people-to-people exchange, and to help our two great countries understand each other and cooperate more. Thank you.

Huiyao Wang: Thank you, Minister Zhu. Now we will have a few final words from John, we'd really appreciate your final comments.

John Thornton: There's so much to say, I'll try to be very succinct. I was admiring the efforts on the part of Jeff Bezos, Richard Branson, Elon Musk, and others to go to space. If you can imagine being on those space-ships looking down on the planet, when you're up there looking down, there's no difference between people living in China, people living in the US, and people living in Africa. I think that we need to hold ourselves to a higher standard and be more conscious of the fact that we live on one planet and the issues are only going to get more complicated and more complex as we go forward. The US and China, which are the two leading countries now and will be for a very long time, have a very big burden. The burden is that they are responsible to lead the world to a safer and better place. Therefore, when we talk about competition and cooperation, I can understand and be comfortable with both of those ideas between the countries. But when we add the idea of confrontation, to me, that's absolutely out of the question and we shouldn't even be considering that as a concept. The world simply can't take it. We shouldn't waste any time on it. As I said in my earlier comments, should the leading countries of the world really be spending their time arguing and trying to do each other down, or should they be spending their time trying to get the world to a better place? To me, the answer is very obvious. And the sooner we recognize that the better. We have a right to demand of our leaders that they get the big things right, as Nixon, Mao, Kissinger, and Zhou Enlai did 50 years ago. Thank you.

Huiyao Wang: Thank you, John. You talked about the recent space trips and looking down to the Earth from outer space to see that we are all really one. I remember the 2008 Beijing Olympics' slogan was "One World, One Dream." This year, the Tokyo Olympics enriches the Olympics motto "Faster, Higher, Stronger" by adding "Together." I think it's great we are adding this new dimension. I really appreciate your time and I look forward to continuing our conversation, as we have at the Wilson Center in the past, and as we hope to do with the Peterson Institute, Brookings, and the Asia Society. So once again, I thank all of you, thank our viewers and we appreciate our speakers' time. Thank you all very much.

China–US Relations in a Multipolar World

A Dialogue with Kishore Mahbubani

Huiyao Wang and Kishore Mahbubani

On October 18, 2021, CCG hosted a dialogue between CCG President Huiyao Wang and Kishore Mahbubani, Distinguished Fellow at the Asia Research Institute, National University of Singapore.

In many ways, Kishore is the ideal discussant to conclude this section on great power relations and this book as a whole. His diverse experience and distinguished career have given him a unique perspective and special insights into the evolving China–US relationship. He is in the rare position of being extremely well informed about both countries but also being a neutral third-party observer, so he is well-placed to help clear the thick fog of misunderstanding that has enshrouded ties between the world's two largest economies.

For over three decades, Kishore Mahbubani served as a diplomat for Singapore, a country with deep ties to both China and the US. In addition to postings around the world, he was twice Singapore's Ambassador

H. Wang (✉)
Center for China and Globalization (CCG), Beijing, China

K. Mahbubani
Asia Research Institute of National University
of Singapore (NUS), Singapore, Singapore

© The Author(s) 2022   187
H. Wang and L. Miao (eds.), *Understanding Globalization,
Global Gaps, and Power Shifts in the 21st Century*,
https://doi.org/10.1007/978-981-19-3846-7_11

to the UN and served as President of the UN Security Council in January 2001 and May 2002. Since then, Mahbubani has gone on to forge a distinguished career in academia, becoming one of Asia's leading public intellectuals and one of the most insightful and eloquent Asian voices on the big issues of our times.

I have known Kishore for over a decade and had the honor and pleasure of discussing and sharing ideas with him in many arenas over the years, most memorably in May 2019, when we debated side by side in one of the "Munk Debates," a mainstage public debate held in Toronto. CCG was also proud to translate one of Kishore's most recent books into Chinese, *Has China Won? The Chinese Challenge to American Primacy*, published in China by CITIC Press. This dialogue also served as a launch event for the Chinese edition of this book, which has attracted considerable attention both in China and abroad. Aside from key topics Kishore covers in that book, our conversation also covers prospects for cooperation on climate change and other shared challenges, China's new drive to achieve "Common Prosperity," economic integration in Asia, and the continuing importance of the UN and other multilateral organizations.

Huiyao Wang: You have played the role of an astute international observer for many years, building bridges between East and West. The Chinese translation of *Has China won? The Chinese challenge to American primacy* was recently published by CITIC Press Group. The book offers a comprehensive and sober analysis of China–US relations and provides suggestions for both countries from your view as a third-party observer. Could you please tell us a bit about what sparked your interest in writing this book and about your views on China–US relations?

Kishore Mahbubani: The reason I wrote the book is that if you can imagine two trains coming down the same track, gaining momentum, and heading toward a collision, what do you do? Do you say, "carry on, have a collision" or do you say "stop, and think twice about whether you really want this collision?".

Unfortunately, the US has launched a geopolitical contest against China. As a result, the US and China are racing toward a collision like two trains. My goal is to try and stop the worst-case scenario of an all-out collision between these two trains. I tried to analyze the reasons why this is happening in my book. They are primarily structural reasons; it is not due to personalities. Many people think that the US–China contest started because of Donald Trump. But you will notice in the first paragraph of my book, I say that while the US–China contest was launched by Donald Trump, it will outlast him. It doesn't matter who the US president is. Sure enough, after Joe Biden became president, he couldn't change anything. The contest will still continue, and even though Biden said in his election campaign that Trump's tariffs are hurting the American people and workers, he cannot remove them, because the geopolitical contest is driven by structural forces. That is the main reason why I wrote this book, to try to explain the structural forces that are driving this contest. Let me quickly outline the reasons.

One is of course the fact that whenever the world's number one emerging power, which today is China, is about to overtake the world's number one power, the US, the world's number one power will always try to push down the world's number one emerging power. So, when the US is trying to prevent China from succeeding, that's normal behavior. That's what all great powers do.

But the second structural reason, that nobody talks about, is that there is also a fear of the "yellow peril" in the Western imagination. This is something that is politically incorrect to discuss in many Western circles, but it's a fact in Western history. In the late nineteenth century, the US Congress passed a bill called the US Chinese Exclusion Act to keep out Chinese immigrants. That reflects the fear of the "yellow peril" that exists in the American psyche, as well the Western psyche.

There's also a third structural factor. That was a bipartisan consensus in the US, among both Republicans and Democrats, that after the US engaged China and opened up to China economically, China would also open up politically, become a liberal democracy, and then the liberal democracy of China and the liberal democracy of US would live happily ever after. As you know, that's a fairy tale, but that's what Americans believed. Because of that, they are very disappointed that China is not creating a political system that Americans like. This is another reason why the US–China geopolitical contest is gaining momentum. So, there are structural reasons why this is happening, and it's not due to personalities. I hope my book could make a contribution to help people understand why all this is happening.

Huiyao Wang: Thank you. I think that's a great rationale for writing this book and to highlight the structural problems, what Graham Allison calls the Thucydides Trap, and as you mentioned, the fear of the "yellow peril," and the misguided bipartisan consensus that China would converge with the US.

Historically, Chinese people have been relatively peace-loving and have generally not colonized other places. As mentioned in your book, Zheng He in the Ming Dynasty actually traveled as far as Africa, but never occupied any colony. That was 100 years before Columbus discovered America.

Looking ahead, how do you think China–US relations will unfold? As Martin Wolf and I discussed, we need to manage the geopolitical risks of China–US frictions. The structural problems will not go away in the next five to ten years. But as Joseph S. Nye Jr. and I discussed, maybe by around the year 2035 we can hope to see some degree of normalization.

What do you think of this time horizon? How long are we going to have this kind of friction, and will we be able to keep it to a manageable level so that we don't get into a "hot war" over the issue of Taiwan or anything related to the South China Sea?

Kishore Mahbubani: These are very good questions. I have a chapter of the book devoted to the question, "is China expansionist?" Of course, I cite the example of Admiral Zheng He, who traveled all the way from China to Africa. He could have conquered many territories and many countries, but he never did. So, this idea that the West has that China is expansionist is not true. If the Chinese were expansionists, then Australia would be a Chinese colony and not a British colony, because Australia is much closer to China than it is to Great Britain.

At the same time, I'm glad that you mentioned Martin Wolf and Joseph S. Nye Jr., and how they said that we've got to find the ways and means to manage the US–China geopolitical contest. I agree with them and that is the conclusion of my book—I say that the paradox about the US–China geopolitical contest is that it is both inevitable and avoidable. It is avoidable, because at the end of the day, if the goal of the US is to improve the well-being of its people, and if the goal of China is to improve the well-being of its people, they should be working together rather than working against each other. That's why I wrote my book, so I agree with your argument.

At the same time, I have been in the US now for eight days and the mood in the US is very anti-China. I have met many Americans who say to me directly and openly that China is the enemy. I was quite shocked, as even though I have written a book about US–China relations, since I did the research for my book, there has been a tremendous shift against China in the American body politic, which I think is very sad.

I actually believe that there is no reason why the US should regard China as its enemy. China is not trying to conquer the US. China is not sending naval vessels to California. China is not sending armies to the Mexican border or the Canadian border to invade the US. Yet so many American people in the US believe that China is the enemy. The people you have interviewed [in this dialogue series]—like Joseph S. Nye Jr., Martin Wolf, and Tom Friedman—I know they all want to achieve a reasonable outcome. But at the end of the day, it's the politicians who have to make the decision.

As I said, even though Biden himself said that Trump's tariffs and sanctions have hurt the American people, he still cannot remove them. And [US Trade Representative] Katherine Tai, I was hoping in her [recent] speech that she would say that [the US] would lift some of the tariffs and sanctions because they hurt the American people, but she can't do it. The mood in the US today is so anti-China that I'm personally very frightened by it. I had no idea how much the mood against China had become so negative in the US, and that's why we need to have this dialogue, to prevent the worst-case outcome from happening between the US and China.

Huiyao Wang: In your book, you wrote that the ultimate concern is not whether America or China wins, but that humanity has to win. We are now facing the pandemic but have not really got our acts together to cooperate, which is a great concern. As you said, there is a growing consensus in the US that China is some kind of an "evil empire." How can we correct that way of thinking?

Kishore Mahbubani: I think you are quite right that many Americans have already begun to see China as the "evil empire." We must in one way or another challenge that perception, but that requires a lot of effort. Actually, I believe that the rest of Asia must speak out more strongly to the fact that the US–China geopolitical contest is not just damaging the US and China, but also the rest of the world.

COVID-19 and climate change are common challenges that we must work together on. You mentioned the last part of my book, where I say that this is not a question of whether China or the US has won, but it's a question of whether humanity has won.

On the same page, I write that humanity thinks it is much smarter than apes living in the forest. But for apes who live in the forest, if the forest is burning, the stupidest thing they could do is continue fighting. They should come together to put out the fire in the forest. Global warming is basically teaching humanity and asking, are you really the most intelligent species on this planet? If global warming is going to kill human beings, regardless of whether you are in China or the US, Bangladesh or Brazil, Nigeria or Norway, it doesn't matter, as climate change is a common challenge and all of humanity should be coming together. Therefore, we should hit the pause button on this US–China geopolitical contest.

Huiyao Wang: Thank you, Kishore. Since the US–China relationship is the world's most important bilateral relationship, we cannot let it deteriorate too much or enter a more dangerous phase. I think there are a few areas for potential cooperation that we could discuss further.

First, as you mentioned, is climate change. At COP 15 on biodiversity in Kunming [in October 2021,] President Xi pledged CNY 1.5 billion, which is over $230 million, to a biodiversity protection fund for developing countries. […] We know climate change is a huge problem, with extreme weather events becoming more frequent. How can we work together to address this common challenge?

Kishore Mahbubani: You're absolutely right and I'm very happy to hear that President Xi has decided to contribute CNY 1. 5 billion toward the biodiversity challenge. Here, I must say that the tragedy about China is that quite often, on global challenges, China contributes a lot, but is not very good at marketing its contributions. The world doesn't really know what China is doing, and I'll give you three or four concrete examples to prove my point.

Firstly, China is the first country in the world to speak about the concept of "ecological civilization," which means that as you modernize and develop, you must also take care of your environment. [Few people outside of China] have heard of ecological civilization, and this is a tragedy.

Secondly, if you look at why climate change is happening now, it's not just because of new greenhouse gas emissions from China, India, and the rest of Asia. It's also because of the stock of greenhouse gas emissions that Western industrialized countries have emitted since the Industrial Revolution over one or two hundred years ago. Again, that's something most people around the world are not aware of.

Thirdly, China has done so much in terms of reforestation. It's reforesting an area the size of Belgium or bigger [each year], which again, [few people] know about. There have also been other contributions, for example, President Xi Jinping ordered that shark fin cannot be served at official banquets, which saw a drop in the price of shark fin and likely saved a lot of sharks. China has taken many such concrete steps which few people are aware of.

This is why it's very important for China to make a bigger effort to try and explain to the rest of the world what it is doing. I think it's important to make sure this message is conveyed, not necessarily by spokespeople of China, but by friends of China around the world. They shouldn't just deploy Chinese propaganda. They should just tell the facts [about China's contributions].

To cite another big example, if China had decided that it would produce the same number of gasoline cars as the US, that would have been terrible for climate change. But China is now the leader in producing electric cars, which will help save the global environment. China is also a leading supplier of solar power and wind turbines. Again, these facts are underappreciated. I think it's important for China to look for friends who can explain these facts—as I said, not propaganda—just let the facts speak for themselves. That's something that China has not been very good at doing so far, and its why there's so much negative coverage of China in the Anglo-Saxon media.

Huiyao Wang: You're right. These are good concrete examples of the communications challenges that China is facing. On the one hand, China is doing well on the KPIs [key performance indicators] regarding climate change. China has been the largest contributor to the world's gain in green coverage over the last 20 years, accounting for at least 25 percent of the increase, though not many people know this. We need to craft a better narrative for that, but also as you said, also let other people talk about it too rather than just convey it through one channel. President Xi has said that China aims to peak carbon emissions before 2030 and to reach carbon neutrality by 2060. At the UN General Assembly [in September 2021] President Xi said that China would stop financing all coal power plants outside China. The 14th Five-Year Plan sets a target to reduce energy intensity by 13.5 percent and carbon emission intensity by 18 percent. But sometimes these concrete plans are not properly explained to the world.

Moving now to the global supply chain crisis, President Biden recently announced that ports in New York and Los Angeles would operate 24 hours a day, 7 days a week as the US tries to overcome goods shortages. Infrastructure is an area where China does comparatively well, for example, seven of the world's ten largest ports are in China. As you mentioned, China is also a leading producer of new energy vehicles, wind power, solar power, and hydropower. So, is there scope for China and the US to work together on infrastructure, for example, tapping synergies between Biden's B3W initiative and the Belt and Road? More generally, can both sides work together to benefit both countries and the rest of the world, rather than demonizing each other?

Kishore Mahbubani: That's a very noble objective, Henry. I think it can be done. But to achieve global cooperation, you first need to explain to people why global cooperation is important. I wrote a book on global governance called *The Great Convergence*, which was also published in China. In that book, I explain that globalization has shrunk the world, as a result of which, the world has changed fundamentally.

To explain how it has changed fundamentally, I have used what I call the boat analogy. In the past, [when we thought of] 7.8 billion people living in 193 separate countries, it was as though they lived in 193 separate boats. Each boat had a captain and crew to take care of it and the boats were separate. So, if one boat got COVID-19, the other boats would not get COVID-19, because they are different boats—[an infectious disease] could not go from one boat to another.

However, the world has shrunk. Now, although 7.8 billion people may live in 193 separate countries, [we see that] they are no longer on 193 separate boats—rather, they live in 193 separate cabins on the same boat. If we had any doubts about this, they have surely been dispelled by COVID-19. The virus began in one cabin, and it spread around the world, showing how we are all on the same boat.

If we share the same boat, we should take care of our common boat. We now know that if we destroy Planet Earth, we have no alternative. If we destroy the environment, the climate, or the atmosphere of Planet Earth, we cannot go and live on any other planet. We cannot transport 7.8 billion people to Mars or anywhere else. Mars is not inhabitable anyway, maybe except for Elon Musk—he can go and build a small colony for himself there, but the whole of humanity cannot go and live in those places. So, it's important for us to understand that we are now on the same boat and that we have a common destiny and we have common challenges, but this requires a complete change in mindset on the part of policymakers. And herein lies the problem.

For many policymakers, especially many Western policymakers, their concepts of geopolitics come from the nineteenth century. When I talk about the structural forces that explain why the US–China geopolitical contest is continuing, it is because policymakers are applying nineteenth-century geopolitical concepts to the twenty-first century. In the past, when you lived in separate countries, it was as though you were living in separate boats. Now, all of us live in the same boat, so our common interests and common challenges are much more important. Therefore, to achieve cooperation as suggested in your question, [the answer is that] we can all cooperate, but first of all, we must understand why we need to cooperate, and the reason why we need to cooperate is that we're all in the same boat. That's the fundamental reason.

Huiyao Wang: I think that's an excellent metaphor. We are all living on the same planet, in the same "global village," on the same boat. We are now fighting a virus and have to get our collective act together.

One of the challenges that people cite for global cooperation is that [China and the West] have different values, different systems, and different development models, which as you write in your book, have not converged. This has led some people to feel that there is no "us," but rather a "you" and "me" that are fundamentally different.

China has its own development model, which has proven quite successful. Francis Fukuyama has now recognized that [contrary to his earlier claim], we have not reached "the end of history." Do you think the West will be able to accept China's Asian development model, such that it doesn't think that China is an "evil empire" if it doesn't converge? Can we become a more multipolar, more diversified world in terms of our accepting different values and respecting others' rights to find a way that works for them?

Kishore Mahbubani: Well, that's a very good question. Before I wrote the book *Has China Won?* I wrote a book called *Has the West Lost It?* And back in 1992, I wrote an essay called "*The West and the Rest*" in *The National Interest*.

One of the most arrogant assumptions that the West has had in looking at the world, and you mentioned Francis Fukuyama who wrote an essay called "*The End of History*" in which he sent a sophisticated message, but what all Westerners heard was that the West had succeeded, the West had achieved liberal democracy, and that all the rest of the world now had to copy the West. [According to this view,] the West doesn't have to adapt or change to other cultures or civilizations.

As I said in my book *Has the West lost It?* Francis Fukuyama's essay did a lot of brain damage to the West, because he put the West to sleep precisely at a time when other Asian Civilizations were waking up, including the Chinese civilization, the Indian civilization, and Southeast Asian civilizations. I think it's important for the West to accept the notion that other civilizations will not become carbon copies of the West. That's the most fundamental thing that the West has got to learn to accept. And the strange thing is, even though the West preaches liberalism, liberalism means that you accept different points of view, alternative points of view, but ironically, the liberals in the West cannot accept a world of diverse civilizations and of civilizations that are not carbon copies of the West. China is certainly not going to become a carbon copy of the West, because Chinese civilization is as old or even older than Western civilization. So, China is going to be quite different.

In the case of China, Chinese leaders have to understand Chinese history, Chinese traditions, Chinese culture, and also Chinese strengths and weaknesses. Whenever the central government in China is weak, the Chinese people suffer. When the Chinese central government is strong, the Chinese people benefit, and that's why the last 30–40 years of Chinese history have been the best 30–40 years of Chinese history for the bottom 50 percent in China in 4000 years of Chinese history. That's a remarkable fact about China that many in the West are not aware of. Chinese civilization is now coming back again, after having gone to sleep for almost 200 years. But China has failed to explain the nature of Chinese civilization to the Western audience. They don't understand it at all. Instead, if there's anything negative that they can pick up in a story about China, they'll write about the negative stuff.

Recently, when China cracked down on big tech companies like Alibaba, Tencent, and DiDi, some people in the West said, "OK, China is going after big companies, China is going to destroy itself." Really? Will China destroy itself? Or is China trying to create a society that is not a plutocracy? In my book, I give a whole chapter to the question of why America is weakening itself by becoming a plutocracy. If China decides not to become a plutocracy, that's a positive development for China. This is something again that China finds hard to explain to a Western audience. What China needs to do a better job of is to say, we respect the fact that you in the West want to have a certain kind of society that works better for America, for the West, where you emphasize individual rights more than individual responsibilities. But maybe China wants to have a society that emphasizes individual responsibilities more than individual rights. We have a diverse world, we have two different kinds of social models. Let each society choose its own social model, and let's see which is the best, instead of saying that "the West is best" and "the rest must copy the West." That's what the West has been saying, but [the Western model] may not necessarily be what is good for other societies. This is what China needs to explain in a very careful and nuanced fashion. But so far, it has not succeeded in explaining to the West that actually, China will never become a carbon copy of the West.

Huiyao Wang: I agree and you put it well. I think China tends to emphasize individual responsibilities more than individual rights. That's the Chinese social model, and it has helped China contain COVID-19. We've had quarantine, lockdown, and people stayed at home, sacrificing some individual rights. But this allowed the whole of society to get free of the virus and return to normal. So, in a way, this pandemic has proven that the Chinese way of doing things may not necessarily be as bad as people thought in the West. But you're right, we have to explain better how China works.

Moving on. This year marks the 100th anniversary of the founding of the CPC and also President Xi has announced that China has eliminated extreme poverty. The 800 million people that have escaped poverty in China account for 70 percent of the global reduction in poverty, helping to fulfil the UN 2030 agenda 10 years ahead of schedule. [Former US Secretary of the Treasury] Larry Summers once said at CCG that this is probably something comparable to the Industrial Revolution in Great Britain, or even greater than that.

But China will not stop there and has now proposed another objective, "Common Prosperity." After lifting 800 million people out of extreme poverty, attention turns to the working class, like DiDi drivers, delivery workers, and the 250 million migrant workers working in different parts of China. Premier Li has noted that around 600 million people earn CNY 1000 a month. So, now the government is focusing its efforts on those less wealthy and less affluent, exactly to avoid the problem that you mentioned in your book about the situation in the US, where the wealth of the top 1 percent is maybe equal to that of 50 percent of the general population, many of whom haven't seen any real progress in the last several decades.

You also mentioned that the government is trying to address the monopolies of big companies and also trying to make things fairer. Recently, there has also been a crackdown on extreme after-school study activities, as this places too much burden on elementary or high school students.

I think there are a lot of ways the central Chinese government is trying to push for noble objectives. By 2035, China is going to be well on its path to basically achieving modernization, and by 2049 becoming a fully modernized and developed society. So, what do you think about this Common Prosperity goal that China has shifted to?

Kishore Mahbubani: In the West, there are two schools of thought on Common Prosperity and what China is trying to do with it. The Anglo-Saxon view is that China is shooting itself in the foot with Common Prosperity, because when China goes after the big tech companies like Alibaba, Tencent, DiDi, when China restricts the power and influence of big companies, China is only ensuring that American big tech firms will succeed and win. So, some people in the Anglo-Saxon world will celebrate the fact that China is going after all these big tech companies. That's one school of thought.

But the other school of thought, which is what I suppose is the view in China, is that these companies in some ways have become too powerful and are putting the interests of [themselves] ahead of the interests of society in many areas. For example, video games may be bad for the population at large and too much tuition may be bad for society at large. So, what China is trying to do is some kind of societal correction, which may actually help the Chinese people and help Chinese families and maybe may result in [increased fertility], if you create a more balanced society for people, especially at the bottom.

So, right now, there are two schools of thought on what Common Prosperity means. Only time will tell which school is right, but I think at the same time, it's very courageous for the Chinese government to take on some of these big tech companies, because China may end up hurting itself in the process. So, it's got to be done very carefully and it's got to be handled in such a way that on the one hand, common prosperity spreads in China, but on the other hand, you have got to make sure that China's global economic growth doesn't slow down. These are contradictory objectives that have to be handled well.

Huiyao Wang: Yes, we need to strike a balance. On the one hand, we need to maintain economic vitality and entrepreneurship for market forces to be strong. On the other hand, we also need to raise the living standards of the working class in China and protect migrant workers. I think China has made a lot of progress in this area. For example, China now has 1 billion people with social security benefits and 1.3 billion people with some form of medical care protection—that's probably the largest such system in the world. To improve on this and expand the middle class is, as you said, a very bold initiative. But if it can be handled well, [Common Prosperity] could help to avoid the polarization in society that we see in some other countries, and help keep populism and nationalism at bay, so that it doesn't disrupt the whole of society. That's the progress China is making and that's my understanding of Common Prosperity.

Now, I'd like to shift to another area. At the end of last year, we saw a big shift with the change of US administration from Trump to Biden. During this time, RCEP has been concluded, and China is also in the process of ratifying a big agreement with the EU on investment. After President Xi mentioned that China is positively considering joining CPTPP last year, this year, the Chinese Minister of Commerce announced that China has officially applied to join CPTPP.

In this context, how do you see rising Asian prosperity? ASEAN has already become China's the largest trading partner and we are seeing the rise of the region as a whole. You have written another book, *The Asian 21st Century*, which CCG is translating and will be published by CITIC. How do you see the rise of Asia, its implications, and the influence of East Asian culture in particular? And how will this impact these new trade schemes?

Kishore Mahbubani: It is quite surprising that in the past, the number one champion of free trade agreements by far used to be the US. I remember in 1985, I accompanied the then-Prime Minister of Singapore Mr. Lee Kuan Yew when he addressed a joint session of the US Congress. This was 36 years ago, and in that speech, Prime Minister Lee Kuan Yew mentioned how the US, by championing free trade and by spending the virtues of free trade, had helped to generate global prosperity. At that time, it was the US that wanted to sign free trade agreements with everybody. I think that in 1985, China had not signed a single free trade agreement. What's amazing is that today, the roles have reversed in a very profound way, such that today the US Congress is not willing to sign or ratify any free trade agreement.

You mentioned the CPTPP. It was President Obama who signed the Trans-Pacific Partnership (TPP), but the US Congress and Senate did not ratify it, which was a tragedy. Now, it's China that wants to join [the successor of the TPP, the] CPTPP. It shows how much the world has changed, so it's very important that we in East Asia continue to promote free trade.

On the question of free trade, I'm glad you mentioned that the RCEP has been concluded. I see many Asian countries delayed the conclusion of the RCEP because they were very keen to get India to join. I must say I felt very sad that at the last minute India decided not to join the RCEP, because by not joining the RCEP, India is not participating in the great growth and success story of East Asia. But we in East Asia must continue to push for greater trade liberalization because the theory of comparative advantage that Ricardo devised is still valid and alive today.

Even though countries like the US or India and others have walked away from the virtues of free trade, we in East Asia must continue to push for it, because trade not only generates economic prosperity, it also generates peace. One of the things I have launched recently, which you can Google and find, is the Asian Peace Program (APP). If you go to our website, what we're trying to do is to generate peace in East Asia, and we believe that one good way of generating peace in East Asia is through encouraging greater free trade and encouraging more free trade agreements. I have written about that in several different places, so I hope that we in East Asia should not just support the RCEP, but should also welcome China's application to join the CPTPP.

Huiyao Wang: I think that's great news. China is now actively pursuing CPTPP membership.

You are an expert on Asia and have been studying and researching this fast-growing continent for a long time. But the region also faces geopolitical risks with rivalry over the South China Sea and the issue of Taiwan. ASEAN has been caught in the middle of the US–China rivalry in the region. Japan, for example, is quite allied with the US. But I'm glad to see that recently Present Xi spoke to the Prime Minister of Singapore and also the new Prime Minister of Japan. So, what do you see as the solution to South China Sea issues with ASEAN countries, and the Taiwan issue? Also, what about ASEAN countries taking sides if there's serious geopolitical conflict? What's your advice for the region?

Kishore Mahbubani: You are right. There are many difficult issues in our region and the reason why my colleagues in the Asia Research Institute of the National University of Singapore and I launched the Asian Peace Program is that there are many geopolitical flashpoints in East Asia, including the South China Sea, Taiwan, and others. What we must do is send a message that even though we continue to have differences over many of these issues like the South China Sea, we will not go to war over them. We try to negotiate peacefully to arrive at an understanding. For example, the ASEAN countries and China are trying to reach an agreement on a code of conduct [for the South China Sea]. This is [an area where] we should push harder and harder to get an agreement, to ensure that there's no conflict in the South China Sea.

I think we can avoid war in the South China Sea, but I'm not so optimistic that we can avoid war in Taiwan, because Taiwan is a much more sensitive issue for China. China believes that Taiwan has always been a part of China and should at one point in time reunify with China, and of course, all of us are hoping for a peaceful reunification between Taiwan and China. But for that to happen, it's important that no parties violate the One-China Policy that has been agreed upon by everybody. And this is what worries me about the Trump administration. Because in the Trump administration, Secretary of State Mike Pompeo tried to walk away from the One-China Policy and that's very, very dangerous. Once you walk away from the One-China Policy, you may trigger a war across the Taiwan Strait, and a war across the Taiwan Strait—if the US gets involved—may lead to a nuclear war. Millions of people would die in a nuclear war, so people need to understand that the stakes on Taiwan are very high and it could lead to the very dangerous outcome of a nuclear war. The best way to avoid a nuclear war is not to change the status quo on Taiwan. We must all respect the One-China Policy and this is something that, for example, most Asian countries respect, and so we must all speak out and explain to Western countries why the One-China Policy is important, and why they should not go back on agreements that were negotiated very carefully between the US and China over the past 50 years since Henry Kissinger went to China in July 1971.

Huiyao Wang: I think the three communiqués are important cornerstones of the China–US relationship. We should maintain that and not change the status quo, in order to avoid military conflict, that's very important.

This year is the 50th anniversary of China resuming its seat in the UN, the 30th anniversary of China joining APEC, and the 20th anniversary of China joining the WTO. These milestones symbolize China's openness to the rest of the world. In your book, you mention that when the Bretton Woods system was established, there were only 2.5 billion people in the world, and today there are 7.8 billion people. Is global governance falling behind global practice? You worked at the UN for a long time—what can be done to enhance global governance and multilateralism, and how can China play a more responsive and larger role in this process?

Kishore Mahbubani: Thank you, a very good question. As you mentioned, I was an ambassador to the UN for over 10 years. [Through this experience,] I fell in love with the UN and think it is one of the most wonderful organizations in the world, and the UN Charter is one of the most beautiful documents in the world. We should work together to try to strengthen the UN.

One of the mistakes that the West has been making, and I documented this in my book, *The Great Convergence*, is that even though the West created all these multilateral institutions, including the United Nations and affiliated organizations like the World Health Organization and the World Trade Organization, over the past 30–40 years, the West has been trying to weaken these organizations. I keep emphasizing that this is against Western interests. The West represents a minority in the global village, and so it is wise for the West to strengthen institutions of global governance in a global village. So, I hope that China will do the exact opposite of what the West is doing when it comes to the United Nations and for a start, I think China should try to revive the United Nations General Assembly. Because the United Nations General Assembly, at the end of the day, represents what I call the parliament or the "National People's Congress" of humanity. China should do its best to go to the United Nations General Assembly and debate many of these global issues.

When the US invaded Iraq, [it] said they were doing something which is in accordance with international law. But all you had to do is to have a debate in the UN General Assembly and let all the countries speak out, and most of the countries would say this is not in accordance with international law. In fact, as Kofi Annan said, since the US' invasion of Iraq was neither an act of self-defense nor endorsed by the UN Security Council, it was illegal under international law, and that's something that the UN General Assembly can say.

So, I hope that China will do its very best to try and revive, strengthen, and support the United Nations. Because the United Nations may become, at the end of the day, a valuable soft line of defense for China, because any time the West attacks China, China can take the issue to the UN General Assembly and then ask the rest of the world, do you agree with the West or do you agree with China? Have a debate, and then the West will be surprised to discover that many in the world don't agree with many points the West is making on global governance issues, and so this provides a geopolitical opportunity for China to strengthen these institutions of global governance like the United Nations.

Huiyao Wang: Thank you for that sound advice. China should attach more importance to the UN, which I think they're already doing now. China has already become the second-largest donor to the United Nations and contributes the most troops to UN peacekeeping forces among the P5 [UN Security Council's five permanent] member countries.

Now we face new issues and challenges such as climate change and the digital economy. Maybe we need new institutions to address international data, carbon, or climate change. There is a need for new multilateral structures and I hope that China can be more actively involved in developing these. Half a century has passed with China in the UN system, which I think is still the cornerstone of world peace and prosperity. As you said, China should really be more active there and have debates in the UN "global parliament," which is the right way to describe it.

We have had a very fascinating discussion. It's quite late now in New York so thank you so much for taking the time to talk to me. We have covered many issues, including China–US relations, which is one of the main themes of your book, as well as climate change, global governance, the United Nations, ASEAN, and Asia. So once again, I want to thank you very much and hope to see you at CCG next time you are in China.

Kishore Mahbubani: Let me also quickly just thank you very much for inviting me to this dialogue. I share your hope that we will have this dialogue once again. I hope next time we will do it in person together face-to-face rather than virtually. Let's hope that day will come very soon. Thank you very much.

Index

© The Editor(s) (if applicable) and The Author(s) 2022
H. Wang and L. Miao (eds.), *Understanding Globalization, Global Gaps, and Power Shifts in the 21st Century*,
https://doi.org/10.1007/978-981-19-3846-7

GPSR Compliance

The European Union's (EU) General Product Safety Regulation (GPSR) is a set of rules that requires consumer products to be safe and our obligations to ensure this.

If you have any concerns about our products, you can contact us on ProductSafety@springernature.com

In case Publisher is established outside the EU, the EU authorized representative is:

Springer Nature Customer Service Center GmbH
Europaplatz 3
69115 Heidelberg, Germany

The manufacturer's authorised representative in the EU is Springer Nature Customer Service Centre GmbH, Europaplatz 3, 69115 Heidelberg, Germany. If you have any concerns regarding our products, please contact ProductSafety@springernature.com

Printed and bound by CPI Group (UK) Ltd, Croydon, CR0 4YY
29/04/2026
02099470-0002